Irish Big Houses

Published in 2009 by
Appletree Press Ltd
The Old Potato Station
14 Howard Street South
Belfast BT7 1AP

Tel: + 44 (28) 90 24 30 74
Fax: + 44 (28) 90 24 67 56
Email: reception@appletree.ie
Web-site: www.appletree.ie

Copyright © Appletree Press Ltd, 2009
Text by Terence Reeves-Smyth
Additional text by Appletree Press
Photographs © as acknowledged on p127

First published as *Irish Country Houses* by Appletree Press in 1994

All rights reserved. Printed in China. No part of this publication may be reproduced, stored in a retrieval system or transmitted in any form or by any means, electronic, mechanical, photocopying, recording or otherwise, without the prior permission of the copyright holder.

A catalogue record for this book is available from the British Library.

Irish Big Houses

ISBN-13: 978 1 84758 118 1

Desk & Marketing Editor: Jean Brown
Editorial work: Jim Black
Designer: Stuart Wilkinson
Production Manager: Paul McAvoy

9 8 7 6 5 4 3 2 1

AP3597

Irish Big Houses

Terence Reeves-Smyth

Westport House, Co. Mayo

Contents

Introduction 7

Irish Big Houses

County Armagh
Ardress 8
The Argory 12

County Clare
Mount Ievers Court 17

County Cork
Bantry House 20
Fota House, Arboretum and Gardens 24

County Down
Castle Ward 29
Mount Stewart 35

County Dublin
Malahide Castle 41
Newbridge House 45

County Fermanagh
Castle Coole 49
Florence Court 55

County Galway
Kylemore Abbey 60

County Kerry
Muckross House 63

County Kildare
Castletown House 68

County Leix
Emo Court 75

County Londonderry
Springhill 80

County Louth
Beaulieu 85

County Mayo
Westport House 89

County Roscommon
Clonalis House 95
Strokestown Park House 97

County Sligo
Lissadell House 101

County Waterford
Lismore Castle 106

County Westmeath
Belvedere 110
Tullynally Castle 115

County Wicklow
Russborough 120

Acknowledgements 127

Index 128

Bantry House, Co. Cork

Introduction

Once standing at the focus of Irish social and political life, country houses in Ireland remain a splendid surviving testimony to the confidence and rich culture of generations of Ireland's ruling families. For centuries the 'Big House' drew upon the best craftsmanship and artistic skills that Ireland had to offer. Nowhere else can visitors today so fully appreciate the remarkable quality and distinctive character of eighteenth- and nineteenth-century Irish craft, evidenced by its plaster work, joinery, wrought-iron work and stonework and the artistry of its furniture, pictures, silver, glass, pottery and porcelain. Despite the tragic loss of so many country houses enough remains for us to enjoy this unique legacy of Ireland's past.

This book is designed to provide information on country houses that are open to the public on a regular basis or by appointment. Every effort has been made to provide a representative selection of houses, though inevitably the choice reflects both a personal taste and the constraints of this book. The central idea has been to include enough background information on the history and contents of each house that visitors will gain some impression of what to expect; more detailed guide books are normally available at each property.

The houses in this book are arranged alphabetically on an all-Ireland county basis. Practical information such as location details are given at the end of each entry, as well as the National Grid Reference number (NGR).

COUNTY ARMAGH

Ardress House

Irish country houses that have developed over the centuries have always held a special fascination and charm, and none more so than Ardress House – a modest gentleman farmer's residence with aspirations of grandeur. Originally a seventeenth-century house, it was enlarged with a hotch-potch of extensions at various times between 1780 and 1810 – all cleverly incorporated behind symmetrically composed façades. One of these additions includes a splendid drawing-room that could belong to a sophisticated Dublin town mansion of the period; above all else it gives Ardress its elegance and distinction.

The central portion of Ardress, behind the five centre windows of the front facade, is a two-storey gable-ended house built sometime around 1670 for the Clarke family. It has a rectangular plan and retains its original steeply pitched butt-purlin roof of local oak – a type of roof-timbering that is only known in five other Ulster houses but is characteristic of vernacular roof carpentry techniques found in many seventeenth century box-framed houses in England. Internally the house retains its tripartite plan, with a long, narrow hall flanked by the parlour on the left and the former kitchen to the right.

In 1700 a new kitchen extension was built to the rear of the house and the present oak staircase erected at one end of the former kitchen, while the remaining area, now known as the inner hall, was integrated

Ardress House, Co. Armagh

with the hall by knocking an arch through the wall. The parlour retains its early proportions and now contains some fine Irish furniture, notably an oak and applewood bureau bookcase made locally circa 1725, a walnut chest dating from 1700 and a good regency-period Pembroke table; the Italian marble scagliola chimney-piece was probably installed around 1740.

A door from the parlour leads into the great surprise of the house – the magnificent drawing-room added in 1780 by the Dublin architect George Ensor, brother of the better-known architect John Ensor. George married the heiress Sarah Clarke in 1760 and decided to settle at Ardress with his wife in 1778 upon his retirement as Clerk of Works to the Surveyor General. The new room was decorated by one of the great stuccodores of the age, Michael Stapleton – the great Irish master of the restrained neo-classical plasterwork associated with Adam.

Stapleton's decorative ceiling design at Ardress is among his best works; it comprises intertwining segments of circles embellished by delicate foliage, urn motifs and a central plaque representing Aurora in 'The Chariot of the Dawn'. More classical medallions are arranged symmetrically on the centre of each wall and are festooned with delicate husk chains. The present colour scheme is based on a free interpretation of the pink and green watercolour tints shown in Stapleton's original drawings in the National Library of Ireland. Prior to 1961 the walls were a sharp green with the decorative plasterwork, frieze and ceiling left white. The room's plasterwork is suitably complemented by a pair of neo-classical settees, a pair of gilded torchéres with sphinx heads and two fine commodes.

The house assumed its present appearance after a series of additions between 1790 and 1810, some of which were evidently made by the author George Ensor (1772-1845) soon after he inherited Ardress from his father in 1803. Two bays of windows were added to each end of the front facade in order to impress – an exercise that involved constructing no less than five dummy windows and a partly false front hut which allowed the formation of an elegant garden front with

Ardress House

curved sweeps at right angles to the main façade. New wings were added to the north and east sides, the latter containing the dining-room which curiously was linked to the drawing-room by a colonnade along the garden front and was later removed in 1879.

The room was restored in 1961 and now contains some exceptional furniture, most strikingly a heavily carved grotesque Irish Chippendale side-table and a pair of commodes made in 1759 by Pierre Langlois. Here hangs a fine collection of paintings from Stuart Hall near Stewartstown and now on permanent loan to the National Trust. They include a group of 'Four Seasons' by Theobald Michau, The Road to Calvary by Frans Francken the younger and Christ on the Road to Emmaus signed by J. Myts (1645-64).

Ardress was inherited in 1845 by the third George Ensor who died unmarried in 1879. The property then passed to his nephew Charles Ensor, and later to Charles's son Captain Charles H. Ensor who sold Ardress to the National Trust in 1960. In addition to upgrading the house, the Trust have restored the mainly eighteenth-century farmyard where visitors can inspect a milking shed, dairy, boiler house, forge and threshing barn. There is also an interesting display of old farm implements.

Located 7 miles from Portadown on the Moy Road (B28). NGR: H 914559.

The Argory

There is a touch of the Marie Celeste about The Argory, as if time had stood still a century ago and its occupants might at any moment return from their vanished world, bringing the place to life. The house is neither large nor grand by nineteenth-century standards. Its importance lies in the remarkable survival of its interior which, unique in Ireland, evokes the atmosphere and ambience of late Victorian country house life.

The Argory was built between 1819 and 1824 by Walter McGeough, alias MacGeough, who assumed the additional name of Bond in 'affectionate regard to the family of his deceased grandmother' upon completion of the house. His decision to build a house here was influenced by his father's will. According to its terms only £400 a year was left to the eldest son William; the bulk of the fortune went to the younger son Walter and his three sisters. Rather curiously, the will stipulated that once Walter married he was no longer allowed to live at Drumsill, the family seat outside Armagh, so long as two of his sisters remained unwed. Although one sister died early, Walter judged correctly that the others would remain husbandless and therefore decided to build his own house on lands he had inherited at Derrycaw, overlooking the River Blackwater.

The commission for the new house went to two young Dublin-based architects, John and Arthur Williamson, almost certainly on the personal recommendation of Francis Johnson who was related to Walter's mother. Surprisingly little is known about

The Argory, Co. Armagh

the Williamsons, though it is clear from the style of their work at The Argory that they trained in Johnson's office. Most of the original plans and accounts relating to the building were lost in 1898 when a fire broke out in the octagonal pavilion, but it is known that the house was originally designed as a single block with the north wing added later. The Argory has imposing ashlar-faced elevations in a restrained classical style. The centre of its two-storey seven-bay west front breaks forward under a shallow pediment and contains a porch whose doorcase is framed by an elliptical arch and embellished with a squashed fanlight, glazed side panels and a lion's mask. This leads directly into the staircase hall, which once served as the front hall until the 1830s when the main entrance overlooking the river was shifted to the less exposed east side, where a small portico was added.

The staircase hall, or west hall, has been described as one of the most exciting interiors of its date in Ireland. It has a theatrical cantilevered staircase with brass banister supports, marbled walls, colza-oil lamp (converted to gas in 1906) and a large cast-iron stove surmounted by a replica of the Warwick vase. The original 1821 drawings of this stove survive; its flue descends beneath the floor to the drawing-room chimney. The room also has an almost life-size bronze cast of a mastiff, one of two bronzes of dogs which date from 1835 and are early examples of the work of the French animalier Charles Fratin.

The decorative scheme of the staircase hall with its marbled walls is continued upstairs in the organ gallery – a broad landing extending through the width of the house with tripartite 'Wyatt windows' at each end. Wilkie prints in ornate gilded frames hang at the staircase end, while at the other stands the very large cabinet barrel organ which is generally accepted as the most important of its kind in existence. This recently restored instrument was commissioned in 1822 from the London organ builder James Bishop; it originally had six barrels, Samuel Wesley being consulted in their selection, but now only three survive.

Perhaps the most attractive of the reception rooms at The Argory is the drawing-room, which lay shrouded in dust-sheets from 1939 until 1979. It was remodelled in the 1890s when the windows were lengthened and a small anteroom and cupboard were run into the room making it larger and brighter. The Carrara marble chimney-piece with baseless Doric columns is original, but most of the furnishing of this comfortable room is late nineteenth century. There are rich curtains and upholstery, copies of old masters in gilt frames on the walls, a Steinway rosewood grand piano bought in 1898 and a workbox nearby ready for use. Other items include two pietro duro round tables which came from Drumsill in 1916, one of which is inlaid with butterflies and the other with the quartered coat of arms of MacGeough and Bond. The ormolu colza-lamp was converted to gas in 1906 when an acetylene gas plant was installed in the yard for £257 17s. 6d. – a sum which included all the fittings, such as the wall brackets each side of the overmantel mirror. The Argory has never been lit by electricity, though the National Trust installed carefully concealed power points when they took over the house in 1979.

On the other side of the staircase hall is the dining room. Much of its furniture was acquired from the Glasgow firm of cabinetmakers and upholsterers James Whyte and Son in 1827, notably the chairs around the long table – which is set with family china and silver for tea. Family portraits line the walls as is so often the case in Irish country house dining-rooms, while some of the accessories in the room include two round-topped tables in mahogany adjusted by a system of internal pulleys and two side-tables, beneath which stand plate buckets and a tea caddy; a warming cabinet sits to the left of the fireplace.

Across the central corridor from the dining-room lies the billiard room – a familiar feature of nineteenth century country houses, though it is rare to see one so well preserved as this. The room retains its original early nineteenth-century table by Burroughes & Watts as well as its early accessories, such as its scoreboard, level, cue stand and rests. The masculine feel of the room is emphasised by the warm appearance of the dado, which has been painted to resemble panelling, while the shutters have been grained to imitate walnut veneer. The other major reception room, the study, contains more family portraits, including a striking one of Walter McGeough by Sir Frederick Grant. This room, which continued to be regularly used by W.A.N. MacGeough Bond until his recent death, reveals a cluttered and reposeful scene crammed with an assortment of family acquisitions spanning four generations.

The Argory and most of its contents were given to the National Trust by the late W.A.N. MacGeough Bond in April 1979. Two years later the house was opened to the public following a major restoration, which included work to the stable block, designed in 1820 and surmounted by a cupola with an eight-day striking clock and a handsome weather-vane. The 300-acre demesne park has many pleasant walks.

Located 4 miles from Moy on the Derrycaw Road. NGR: H 872580.

COUNTY CLARE

Mount Ievers Court

Like many of Ireland's tall eighteenth-century houses, Mount Ievers Court has a dream-like, melancholic quality that is positively beguiling. Set in lush parkland and sheltered by beech trees, the house rises three storeys over a basement, its height accentuated by a steeply pitched roof, tall chimney stacks and the subtle architectural devise of reducing the width of each storey by six inches. Each of its seven-bay fronts are almost identical, save one that is of silvery-grey limestone ashlar and the other of brick imported from Holland as ballast and now faded a beautiful shade of pink-grey. Its exquisite doll's house appearance is enhanced by string-coursing, quoins, lugged window surrounds and by small panes and heavy astragals in the window glazing – standard features of early eighteenth-century architecture.

Work began on the house in 1731 when Colonel Henry Ievers demolished the seventeenth-century tower house that his grandfather Henry Ievers had acquired less than seventy years before. A stone fireplace dated 1648 was salvaged from the castle and re-erected in the hall of the house where it still stands. The architect of the new house was John Rothery, whose son Isaac completed the work after his death in 1737. From a complete building account which survives, we know that eleven masons and forty eight labourers were employed – the masons earning five shillings a week and the labourers only five pence, though each received food, drink, clothing and in some cases accommodation. Slates which cost nine shillings six pence per thousand came from Broadford ten miles away, while the massive oak-roof timbers, thirty-four tons in weight, came from Portumna, travelling by boat to Killaloe and hauled the twenty miles overland to Mount Ievers. With so much of the work relying on local labour and materials the cost of the house was only £1,478 7s. 9d. This was a comparatively small amount by the standards of the time.

The interior of the house has a simple, restrained feel. Many rooms retain their contemporary panelling, including several in plaster that directly follow the lines of wood panelling. The ceilings, with their geometric panels and modillion cornices in the hall, the staircase and the upper hall are all reminiscent of Carolinian houses, as is the magnificent staircase with its fine joinery of alternate barley-sugar and fluted balusters. On the top floor is a long gallery possibly designed as a ball-room, a feature that is unique in Ireland – though Bowenscourt in County Cork once boasted one, a house also built by Isaac Rothery but tragically now demolished. The lovely chimney-pieces throughout the house, which include a Bossi, were installed around 1850 and are mostly late Georgian though the grates seem to be original to the house.

Other striking features include the fine brass knocker on the front door, the vaulted basements and a delightful 1740's fresco in the drawing-room giving a panoramic view of the house, demesne and landscape beyond. The formal garden landscape around the

Mount Ievers Court

house has now largely disappeared, although the present owner, has restored the fish ponds represented in the fresco. He has also given the house a new roof and has done much to ensure that this magical building will survive into the next century.

Located just outside of Sixmilebridge, north east of Limerick. NGR: R 487663.

COUNTY CORK

Bantry House

Bantry House is a theatrical place, full of drama and character. Standing at the foot of a steep terraced garden, it commands incomparable views across the waters of Bantry Bay to Whiddy Island and the Caha Mountains beyond. Its magnificent setting, like a Claude Lorraine painting, is matched by the many treasures of its interior – exquisite French furniture, tapestries and objets d'art – which give this remote Irish house the air of a continental baroque palace.

The original house, a five-bay three-storey building, was built by Samuel Hutchinson around 1690; called Blackrock, it forms the nucleus of the present Bantry House. In 1760s it was acquired by Richard White, a farmer from Whiddy Island who had amassed a fortune from pilchard-fishing, iron-smelting and probably from smuggling. Through a series of purchases, he acquired most of the land around Bantry including large parts of the Beare Peninsula – estates which were further enlarged by his grandson Richard White (1767-1851). The young Richard took little interest in social or political affairs, preferring to live quietly at Bantry, but in December 1796 he was unexpectedly thrust into the limelight when a French invasionary fleet sailed into Bantry Bay to join forces with the United Irishmen. White showed great initiative during the crisis by organising local defences and placing his home, then called Seafield, at the disposal of General Dalrymple who arrived with troops from Cork.

Bantry House, Co. Cork

Months after the would-be invasion, Richard White was created Baron Bantry in 1797 in recognition of his 'spirited conduct and important service' during the crisis; in 1801 he was made a viscount and in 1815 became the Earl of Bantry.

Although some modifications appear to have occurred during the 1770s, most of the additions and alterations took place during the first Earl's lifetime. A two-storey addition with bowed ends and a six-bay front facing onto Bantry Bay were added in 1820, providing space for two large drawing-rooms and several bedrooms above. Many more substantial changes were made in 1845 by Richard, viscount Berehaven (1800-67) – a passionate art collector who travelled regularly across Europe, visiting Russia, Poland, France and Italy and bringing back shiploads of exotic goods between 1820 and 1840. To accommodate his new furnishings, the Viscount built a fourteen bay block to the rear of the old house consisting of a six-bay centre of two storeys over a basement flanked by four-storey bow-ended wings. No doubt inspired by the grand baroque palaces of Germany, he gave the house a sense of architectural unity by lining the walls with giant red-brick pilasters with Coade-stone Corinthian capitals, the intervening spaces consisting of grey stucco and the parapet adorned with an attractive stone balustrade. He also laid out the Italianate gardens, including the magnificent terraces on the hillside behind the house, most of which was undertaken after he had succeeded his father as the second Earl of Bantry in 1851. After his death in 1867 the property was inherited by his brother William, the third Earl (1801-84), his grandson William, the fourth and last Earl (1854-91), and then passed through the female line to the present owner, Mr Shelswell-White.

Today, Bantry House remains much as the second Earl left it, with an important part of his great collection still intact. Nowhere is this more so than in the hall where visitors will find an eclectic collection garnered from a grand tour which includes an Arab chest, a Japanese inlaid chest, a Russian travelling shrine with fifteenth- and sixteenth-century icons and a Friesian clock. There is also a fine wooden seventeenth-century Flemish overmantel and rows of family portraits on the walls. The hall was created by combining two rooms with the staircase hall of the original house and consequently has a rather muddled shape, though crisp black-and-white Dutch floor tiles lend the room a sense of unity. Incorporated in this floor are four mosaic panels collected by Viscount Berehaven from Pompeii in 1828 and bearing the familiar inscriptions 'Cave Canem' and 'Salve'. Other unusual items on show include a mosque lamp from Damascus in the porch and a sixteenth-century Spanish marriage chest which can be seen in the lobby.

Undoubtedly the most spectacular room in the house is the dining-room, dominated by copies of Allan Ramsay's full-length portraits of George III and Queen Charlotte whose astonishingly elaborate gilt frames are well set off by the royal blue walls. The ceiling was once decorated with Guardi panels, but these have long since been removed and sold to passing dealers at a fraction of their worth. The differing heights of the room are due to the fact that they are partly incorporated in the original house and in the 1845 extension, their incongruity disguised by a screen of marble columns with gilded Corinthian capitals. Much of the furniture has been here since the time of the second Earl, including the fine George III dining table, Chippendale chairs, mahogany teapoy, immense sideboards made especially for the room and the enormous painting The Fruit Market by Snyders revealing figures reputedly drawn by Rubens

– a wedding present to the first countess.

The first flight of the staircase from the hall belongs to the original early eighteenth-century house, as does the half-landing with its lugged architraves. This leads into the great library, built around 1845 and the last major addition to the house. The library is over sixty feet long, has screens of marble Corinthian columns, a compartmented ceiling and Dublin-made marble mantelpieces at each end with overhanging mirrors. The furnishing retains a fine rosewood grand piano by Bluthner of Leipzig, still occasionally used for concerts. The windows of this room once looked into an immense glass conservatory, but this has now been removed and visitors can gaze out upon the restored gardens and the steep sloping terraces behind. Visitors can even stay overnight at Bantry House as accommodation is available in the house on a bed and breakfast basis.

Located on the outskirts of Bantry on the N71. NGR: V 988481.

Fota House, Arboretum and Gardens
The demesne of Fota, or Foaty Island, contributes enormously to the beauty of the Lee Estuary whose sublimity moved Lady Chatterton to write in 1838: 'the sun always seems to shine brighter here than elsewhere'. Fota's magnificent parkland, its gardens and splendid mansion – one of Ireland's finest regency houses – combine to create an aura of charm and serenity apparent to all who visit.

Fota House, Co. Cork

Fota's former owners were direct descendants of Philip de Barry, a Norman settler who was granted lands in Cork in 1179. The main branch of this family, the Earls of Barrymore, lived at Barryscourt about one mile east of Fota until 1630 when they moved to Castle Lyons, some fifteen miles to the north. Their great estates were later ruined by the reckless gambling of 'Hellgate', the seventh Earl of Barrymore, but Fota was unaffected by this debacle for it had earlier been given to Arthur, third son of the fourth Earl. In the 1750s Arthur built a five-bay hunting box on Fota and after his death in 1770 the property passed to his wealthy younger brother John, and later in turn to his eldest son James Hugh Smith-Barry of Marbury, Cheshire. James spent much of his time hunting and racing in England, only using Fota occasionally, but his eldest son John, who inherited the property in 1801, had a rather different attitude to his Irish home. John had a passion for sailing and from an early age preferred to live at Fota where he could race with the Royal Cork Yacht Club. As soon as he came of age in 1814 he married an Irish girl from Ballyedmund and decided to make Fota Island his principal seat.

Initially, John Smith-Barry planned to build a new residence on a more elevated site on Fota and commissioned the Irish architect Richard Morrison and his son William Vitruvius to design a mansion in the new Tudor Revival style. This was later rejected and in the early 1820s the Morrisons were engaged to alter and extend the old Georgian box. They added two pedimented wings to either side of the old house, built a Doric portico and remodelled the interior in the rich classical regency style it retains to this day. They also constructed a long two-storey service range to one side of the house and helped to create the park, demesne wall, gatelodges and other demesne buildings. John Smith-Barry, however, did not have long to enjoy his splendid new seat and died in 1837, barely eight years after it was finished. He had lived lavishly, earning him the nickname 'John the Magnificent', but his son James Hugh reacted against this and rarely visited Fota until after his marriage in 1841. Later, James spent more time at Fota where he

Fota House, Arboretum and Gardens

established the famous arboretum, and just before his early death in 1856 he completed the billiard-room wing at the end of the service range – built in the same style as the Morrison wings but with only one storey. In 1872 the engineer Sir John Benson added a billiards room and an extensive conservatory, which was later altered in 1897 to become a gallery. The area between the billiard room and the main building was filled in, during 1890, with a single-storey range containing a long gallery – the inspiration of Arthur Smith-Barry, first and last Lord Barrymore (1843-1925).

Fota was later inherited by Lord Barrymore's son in-law and daughter, Major and the Honourable Mrs Bell, who sold Marbury, the family seat in Cheshire, and moved their valuable picture collection to Fota. Upon the death of Mrs. Bell in 1975, Fota Estate was put on the market and University College Cork purchased the whole estate. Part of it was sold and Fota Island Golf Club was developed on the land.

Fota House contains over 70 rooms and of these 60 have fireplaces, ranging in size from the servants' quarters to the large and beautifully proportioned principal rooms. An interesting aspect to Fota house are the 'dummy' windows which were designed to enhance the aesthetic balance of the house. Visitors are often surprised by the wealth of sumptuous decorative detail in the house, for the simplicity of the building's exterior gives no hint of what lies within. The entrance hall takes up the entire front of the old house and is divided by screens of yellow scagliola columns whose Ionic capitals support lintels decorated with wreaths alternating with the Barry crest. The hall extends into anterooms at each end, giving access to the main reception rooms of the house. In the north wing lies the dining-room while to the south are the library and the big drawing-room.

In converting the hunting lodge into a residence, two new wings were added along with a Greek Doric portico entrance. The interior was opened up with fine scagliola columns leading to a stone staircase and the ceilings of the library and drawing room were decorated with great delicacy in the French style. Some of the best plasterwork in the house can be found in the staircase hall opposite the main entrance. The stairs, with their brass banisters, rise beneath an enriched shallow dome, while a pair of columns on the top landing flank an attractive vista to a secondary flight that leads to the top storey.

In 1990, Fota House, Arboretum and Gardens were leased to the Fota Trust and the gardens and arboretum were transferred to the Office of Public Works in 1996. In December 2007, Fota House became the first property acquired by the newly formed Irish Heritage Trust – a charity created in 2006 to care for historic properties, houses and gardens throughout Ireland. This move has undoubtedly safeguarded the future of the house and gardens for generations to come.

Since the Irish Heritage Trust took over responsibility for the property the long process of reinstating its former collections of art and furniture has begun. This was greatly helped in 2008 by the acquistion of the original Smith Barry family portraits together with fourteen prints and four engravings thanks to the Cork-based McCarthy family. This family also generously donated a number of eighteenth and nineteenth century landscape paintings by Jonathan Fisher, Thomas Roberts, Robert Carver and three landscapes by William Ashford. The landscapes represent the type of fine Irish art once common in many of the great Irish houses. In addition, Sir Hugh Smith Barry's Deputy Lieutenant's uniform from the late nineteenth century was donated by an anonymous benefactor. It is hoped that gradually more of the house's former treasures will return to their original home. For further information on the work of the Irish Heritage Trust please visit their website at www.irishheritagetrust.ie

Fota Island is 9 miles from E of Cork City. NGR: W 790715.

COUNTY DOWN

Castle Ward
The walled demesne of Castle Ward and its surrounding estate of around 860 acres lies beside and rises, gently, above Strangford Lough. The estate had been a working farm from the time of the tower house of Old Castle Ward, circa 1610. It had increased in size as the prosperous Wards acquired more land and erected more buildings. These estate buildings include a corn mill. Most of the buildings from the eighteenth and nineteenth centuries remain, apart from the previous

Castle Ward, Co. Down

house of circa 1710. The existing 1770's house was built at the one time in two architectural styles and this is what makes it unique in Ireland.

In this mansion house several interesting aspects of country house design are evident in the decorative treatment of the three floors above basement and either side of the longitudinal axis. As is evident in the ground floor's three front rooms, the interior design and treatment celebrates the Palladian neo-classical façade of the Classical side of the house. This external treatment features a rusticated ground floor and a three-bay pediment featuring engaged

Castle Ward

columns – the choice of Gothick for the other side inevitably meant the creation of a suitable façade to accommodate the pointed windows. The garden front overlooking Strangford Lough is in the Gothick taste with ogee- and centre-pointed windows and a crenellated parapet with pinnacles.

The application of an inspired "Strawberry Hill Gothick" featuring these pointed windows has resulted in an adventurous design, but one that is admired for the materials, details and craftsmanship carried over into this sphere of the building. The architectural treatment of both the internal and the external finishes is impressive. The result of a decision taken by the Wards of the late 1700's, whether a compromise or not, is a fascinating and unique house of interest and contrast. This makes Castle Ward one of the most memorable eighteenth-century houses in Ireland.

Sadly, little documentary evidence has survived relating to the building of the house, though it is clear that work began in 1761 and lasted until 1767. It was commissioned by Bernard Ward, later first Viscount Bangor (1719-81), whose family first settled in the area around 1570 when they built the original Castle Ward – a tower house which stands in the farmyard close to the shore. In 1710 a new mansion was sited beyond this and built in the Queen Anne style by Bernard's father, Judge Michael Ward (1683-1759). He was a remarkable figure who achieved great wealth through marriage and business acumen. His house no longer stands, but much of its surrounding formal landscape survives, notably the impressive Temple Water dug in the 1720s.

Bernard proved to be no less energetic than his father and began creating a 'naturalistic' landscape park as a setting for his new house before his father's death in 1759 – no doubt encouraged by his wife Lady Anne Bligh, daughter of the first Earl of Darnley of Rathmore, County Meath.

Work on the house was well underway when Castle Ward was visited by Mrs Delany in July 1762. (Mrs Delany was married to a friend of Dean Swift, the Rev. Dr. Patrick Delany of Delville, near Dublin. She was a pioneering gardener, an intrepid traveller and a visitor to many of the big houses of Ireland.) Her expression of concern that the new house 'should not be judiciously laid out', is often quoted along with her reference to the 'whimsical Lady Anne Ward'. Mrs Delany admired the magnificent setting – but doubted the taste and judgement of Lady Anne. The house is seen in a better-informed light today and is appreciated for its uniqueness.

The architect's identity remains a mystery – it is generally accepted that he was not Irish but could have been any one of several dozen competent architects operating in England at that time. His plan was a rectangle with semi-octagonal bays at each end, the façades being built of Bath stone which Bernard had used when erecting Lady Anne's Temple around 1750.

After Bernard's death in 1781 the estate was placed in Chancery on the illness of the eldest son, Nicholas. Robert, his younger brother was granted a substantial estate along with Bangor Castle but Edward, the second son, moved into the mansion. There was sibling jealousy and mismanagement and the estate deteriorated until Edward's son, Edward Southwell Ward, the third Viscount (1790-1857), refurbished the interior.

The main hall and the original entrance to the house functioned as a music room after 1870. This was after the new entrance porch addition. The original plastered ceiling of the hall is executed in the style of the Italian plasterers working in Dublin during the Georgian period. A screen of scagliola Doric columns, divides the space. A fine marble fireplace surround accommodates a Victorian wood-burning grate and tiled hearth. The late nineteenth-century parquet floor replaced the original seen by Sir James Caldwell on his visit in 1722 and referred to as 'inlaid with oak and mahogany and diced and kept smooth with rubbing and beeswax that you are in danger of slipping every moment'. The most remarkable feature of the room is the wall plasterwork added in 1828 by plasterers from nearby Dundrum, featuring a series of plaster pendants or trophies depicting the interests of the family over the generations.

Two rooms flank the main hall. The library is not an especially distinguished room, though it does house a fine example of an intact collection of books found in the big houses of Ireland. The Irish painter, William Ashford's fine landscape – a view from the temple across the park at Castle Ward, dated 1785 hangs over the fireplace. The Dining Room, which Sir James Caldwell rightly observed was 'quite too small for such a Lady Anne's Templehouse', is an attractive room with nineteenth-century painted, grained and gilded panelling and it has a chimney-piece with a charming relief panel of Ceres and Cupid frolicking amongst vine leaves. Above the fireplace is an unusual 1807 portrait group of figures in an interior and gathered around a table. These include the hon. Edward Ward, painted at the Bishop's Palace at Dromore and the painting is attributed to Thomas Robinson, a pupil of Romney.

The main Gothick room in the house is the saloon in the centre of the east front – most striking for the rich quality of its decoration, with a raised ceiling of fretting and quatrefoils. A Gothick overmantle framing an allegorical painting is mounted over a fine marble fireplace. Off this room is the sitting-room or boudoir housing a collection of Mary Ward watercolours. Mary Ward (1827-69) was associated with Castle Ward. She was born Mary King, the daughter of a rector in Offaly. She was a botanical artist and a naturalist and she published a number of books connected with the microscope. She married Henry Ward in 1854 but died before he succeeded his brother as fifth Viscount in 1881. Looking upward, the room offers the element of surprise because of its spectacular shaped, ribbed and quatrefoil plaster decorated ceiling.

The boudoir is situated adjacent to the main staircase, notable for its elegant wrought-iron balustrade with S-scrolls of the type popularised by Sir William Chambers. The cantilevered staircase occupies a bay in the middle of the north-west façade and gives access to the bedroom floors, the first floor having the showrooms and central corridor. Steps drop down from the lower staircase hall to the mid Victorian entrance porch and from there a single stairway access continues to the basement kitchen and store rooms.

On the death of Henry's eldest son Maxwell Ward, sixth Viscount Bangor (1868-1950), Castle Ward was given in lieu of death duties to the Northern Ireland government and then it was passed on to the National Trust who have continued to maintain and present the house.

Located 1 mile west of Strangford on the Downpatrick Road (A25). NGR: J 573494.

Mount Stewart

Social entertainment was always an important part of country house life and nowhere more so than at Mount Stewart, whose luxuriously appointed and sun-filled apartments were once the setting for a succession of glittering house parties that sometimes even included royalty. The Marquesses of Londonderry were fabulously rich and although they had an English seat and a palatial house in Park Lane, regularly came back to Mount Stewart where they continued their role as prominent political hosts. Their house, a long, low and deceptively large classical building overlooking Strangford Lough, has undergone many changes by successive generations of the family, most recently by Edith, wife of the seventh Marquess, during the

Mount Stewart, Co. Down

interwar years. It retains its comfortable house-party atmosphere, while its famous formal gardens created by Edith as an extension to the reception rooms remain much as she left them.

The Stewarts achieved their enormous wealth largely through astute marriage arrangements. Originally, the family settled near Moville where they had been granted lands in the seventeenth century, but in 1737 Alexander Stewart (1700-81) married Mary Cowan, an heiress with shares in the East India Company. With her fortune he purchased the demesne lands of Mount Stewart in 1744, originally known as Mount Pleasant, and built a house there. His son Robert (1739-1821) consolidated the family's fortune and social influence and was created first Marquess of Londonderry in 1816. He employed James 'Athenian' Stuart to build the Temple of the Winds above Strangford Lough between 1782 and 1785; later, between 1804 and 1806, he engaged the London architect George Dance to design what is now the west wing of the mansion. Nearly two decades earlier Wyatt had been brought in to remodel his father's house, but Wyatt's designs were never to be realised as so much money was spent getting the young Robert Stewart elected as MP for County Down – an election which turned out to be a good investment since Stewart, later Lord Castlereagh and second Marquess of Londonderry (1769-1822), rose to be Foreign Secretary, leader of the House of Commons at Westminster and perhaps the greatest political figure of his generation.

Lord Castlereagh committed suicide in 1822 and the family estates were inherited by his half-brother Charles, the third Marquess (1778-1854). A few years earlier he had married Lady Frances Anne Vane-Tempest, heiress to one of England's richest families with vast estates and collieries in the north of England. Although the new Marquess now found his time divided between a string of country seats in England and the palatial Holderness – later Londonderry House in Park Lane – he nevertheless engaged the celebrated Irish architect William Vitruvius Morrison to rebuild and enlarge Mount Stewart in 1835. The

Irish Big Houses

work was finished around 1840, some two years after Morrison's death, and comprised a large new block to the rear of the old house with an eleven-bay entrance front and pedimented porte cochère. The new work was designed so that it matched Dance's earlier building and a balustraded roof parapet was added to give the whole house a sense of unity.

The main door of the entrance hall leads into the principal interior feature of Morrison's house – a great central hall with an octagonal balustraded gallery lit from above through a dome filled with stained glass. The room now features pieces of sculpture, as it was probably originally intended to, while display cabinets contain a striking Chinese Export armorial service with the arms of Sir Robert Cowan, Governor of Bombay, whose fortune provided the Stewarts with the means to acquire the house in 1744. In mid Victorian times, however, the fourth Marquess (1805-72) had this chamber filled with over 3,000 antlers, a wide variety of animal heads, heraldic banners and suits of armour. By all accounts the fourth Marquess, who undertook an adventurous expedition to the Middle East in 1842, was quite a romantic, it was he who built Scrabo Tower overlooking Newtownards during the 1850s in memory of his father.

A passage from the central hall leads to the core of Dance's earlier house – an imperial staircase with stone treads, wrought-iron balusters and a ramped mahogany handrail. The roof is lit by an octagonal skylight dome with segmental arch supports that is typical of Dance and of his famous pupil Sir John

Soane. Below are large display cases filled with a variety of fine porcelain, part of a large collection at Mount Stewart. The dominant feature of the room however, and perhaps the most important picture in Ireland is the magnificent 'Hambletonian', the masterpiece by George Stubbs that was moved here from Londonderry House during the last war. It depicts a racehorse owned by Sir Henry Vane-Tempest being rubbed down after it had just beaten Joseph Cookson's horse Diamond at Newmarket in 1799.

Adjacent to the staircase hall is the music room which lies at the centre of the west front, flanked by the sitting-room and the Castlereagh room. All three rooms remain very much as Dance had left them, particularly the music room with its delicate ceiling of pendentives and its oak and mahogany floor with central inlaid patera – almost certainly the work of John Ferguson who was responsible for the outstanding marquetry on the floor of the upper room in the Temple of the Winds. The flanking Castlereagh room, originally the dining-room and later the library, has been filled by the National Trust with items relevant to the life and times of Lord Castlereagh – the 'Winston Churchill' of British politics during and after the Napoleonic War.

Morrison's principal reception rooms – the dining-room and the drawing-room – flank the south and north elevations respectively. They are both spacious, long, rectangular rooms, but the dining-room has subsequently been shortened by the incorporation of a kitchen at the east end, beyond a screen of Ionic columns. The room is still impressive, however, and ranged against the walls are the twenty-two Empire chairs which were used by the delegates to the Congress of Vienna in 1815; the backs and seats of the chairs were embroidered by nuns in Nantes for Edith, seventh Marchioness, depicting the arms of those present and the nations they represented. Above the chairs hang life-sized portraits by Sir Godfrey Kneller of the first Earl and Countess of Albermarle, forebears of Lady Mairi Bury's late husband and Edith's son-in-law. King Edward and Queen Alexander would have dined here when they visited Mount Stewart in 1903. One wonders whether the sixth Marquess, in the presence of the King, indulged his famed habit of eating dinner as rapidly as possible – a habit which understandably made him very unpopular with guests whose plates were often whisked away by footmen before they had tasted anything.

The vast drawing-room, with Ionic column screens at each end, remains much as it was after being decorated in the 1930s by Edith, seventh Marchioness, who like her mother-in-law before her was one of the great political hostesses of the time. The furnishing comprises quite a mixture of pieces from different periods, including Carrara marble urns and vases, tripod candlesticks carved with winged lions, standard lamps, sofas, armchairs, occasional tables – all grouped informally as if the house guests were expected to return at any moment. It is perhaps sad that they never will, but the house and its remarkable gardens are now wonderfully maintained by the National Trust for all to enjoy.

Located 5 miles south east of Newtownards on the Portaferry Road (A20). NGR: J 552698.

COUNTY DUBLIN

Malahide Castle

Such was the troubled state of Ireland's past that few Irish country houses were ever continuously inhabited by the same family for more than a few centuries. A rare exception to this rule was Malahide Castle – home of the Talbots for 791 years. Granted in 1185 to Richard Talbot, one of the knights who arrived in Ireland with Henry II in 1174, the property remained in Talbot hands until 1976 when it was acquired by Dublin County Council. Unfortunately, the Irish government was unwilling to accept the property in lieu of death duties, and its remarkable collection of portraits and furniture, which uniquely reflected Ireland's historical and cultural development, had to be sold by auction. Fortunately, Ireland's tourist board, Bord Failte, managed to purchase much of the furniture at the sale together with the castle's carpets and curtains, and these remain at Malahide alongside thirty-five portraits bought by the National Gallery of Ireland. Further important acquisitions of Irish furniture have been added to the collection so that Malahide's interior still retains much of its old beauty and magic.

The core of the medieval castle is the oak room,

Malahide Castle, Co. Dublin

approached by a winding stone staircase and lit by Gothic windows added in 1820 when the room was enlarged and the front hall below was created. The room contains fine carved panelling, mostly of sixteenth-century date, which has darkened to a gleaming ebony. Some of the carving is of Flemish origin, including six exquisite panels representing biblical scenes opposite the window; their religious theme suggests that the Talbots, who remained Roman Catholics until 1774, used this room as a chapel in penal times. According to tradition, Malahide the Flemish carving of the coronation of the virgin over the mantelpiece disappeared when the castle was occupied by the Cromwellian Miles Corbet between 1653 and 1660.

Fortunately for the Talbots, the unsavoury Corbet was one of the regicides who signed the death warrant of Charles I and after the Restoration he was duly hung, drawn and quartered at Tyburn. Samuel Pepys recorded the occasion in his diary on 19 April 1662: 'This morning before we sat, I went to Aldgate and at the corner shop, a draper's, I stood and did see Barkestead, Okey and Corbet drawn towards the gallows.' The Talbots returned to Malahide and the figure of the virgin made a miraculous reappearance above the fireplace. Until 1976 the room contained James Boswell's ebony cabinet in which were found over 1,000 manuscript pages of Boswell's Life of Johnson in the 1920s.

The thick walls of the oak room are flanked on the east side by the great hall, added to the castle around 1475. Unique in Ireland, this great hall not only retained its original form but also remained in domestic use as a dining-room until 1976. Its vaulted undercroft and corbel heads of Edward IV are original, but during the nineteenth century it was given a new roof, mantels and a minstrels' gallery. The furniture and pictures are of mostly seventeenth- and eighteenth-century date. The Talbot ancestral portraits on display were acquired by the National Gallery. This collection of portraits is quite unusual since most of the Talbots' ancestors were Jacobites rather than the supporters of King William who usually decorate Irish country houses.

Irish Big Houses

Some valuable pictures were lost to this room in 1976. In order to replace the lost pictures along the side wall, the National Gallery loaned the huge Battle of the Boyne by Wyck – a superb picture that not only suits this room visually but is historically appropriate; on the morning of the Battle of the Boyne fourteen Talbot cousins, all followers of James II, gathered here to dine – none survived the carnage of the day.

The west side of the castle is occupied by an early seventeenth-century addition which once contained four tapestry-hung chambers. The wing was burnt around 1760 and these rooms were subsequently replaced with two fine drawing-rooms, while externally the architect added round corner turrets, giving the house a Georgian Gothick character. The two rooms were given splendid rococo plasterwork ceilings; the life-like mouldings in the coves of the smaller drawing room are attributable on stylistic grounds to the great Dublin stuccodore Robert West.

Above all, however, these drawing-rooms are famous for their wonderful nineteenth-century painted orange-terracotta walls that many have apparently attempted to reproduce without success over the years. The colour makes an ideal background for the gilt frames of the fine pictures that grace the walls.

The larger drawing-room retains its lovely Chinese carpet and also boasts two French-style gilt settees circa 1770 and a pair of George II Irish giltwood sideboards with black lacquered tops. The sideboards had been acquired at the auction by an international art dealer who was just about to pass them on to an

Iranian client when he was persuaded to sell them back to Malahide. The delightful little turret rooms with ogee Gothic windows beside the two drawing-rooms have long been used to feature small pictures and miniatures. In one hangs a set of Trench family portraits – six pastels and twelve oils by Hugh Douglas Hamilton in frames possibly designed by Gandon.

The famous gardens around the castle are largely the creation of the late Lord Talbot de Malahide who died suddenly in April 1973. They have been well restored by Dublin County Council and are certainly worth visiting. Also in the castle yard is the Cyril Fry Model Railway Exhibition with its model engines, rolling stock and replicas of railway stations in Dublin, Belfast and Cork.

Located in Malahide, 9 miles north of Dublin. NGR: O 220452.

Newbridge House
Although located within a few miles of Dublin's advancing urban sprawl, Newbridge House still manages to preserve its character of a secluded eighteenth century gentleman's residence set in a wooded demesne. The house features a series of beautifully proportioned rooms each retaining their original furnishings thanks to an agreement between the Cobbe family and its new owners, Dublin City Council, who acquired the property in 1986 and have since embarked on a major restoration of the house, yards and parkland.

The front façade of Newbridge is particularly attractive. A facing of pink ashlar gives it a lovely warm glow, while the use of a high basement, solid roof parapet, shouldered window architraves and tripartite doorway within a two-storey six-bay composition is also undoubtedly a success. For many years Newbridge was believed to be the work of Richard Castle, but we now know that it was designed by the prominent British architect James Gibbs and built between 1749 and 1750 for Archbishop Charles Cobbe on land acquired in 1736.

Charles Cobbe (1686-1765) first came to Ireland in 1717 as chaplain to his cousin – the Lord Lieutenant and second Duke of Bolton. Despite a limited intellectual capacity he enjoyed rapid promotion through three minor bishoprics and became Archbishop of Dublin in 1742. His portrait hangs in the hall and shows him wearing a long grey wig and a black sleeveless surplice over the full long sleeves of a bishop. He died in 1765 and the house was inherited by his son Thomas and his fashionable wife, Lady Betty Beresford, sister of the first Marquis of Waterford. They built a wing at the back of the house to accommodate a huge drawing room for entertaining and a gallery to house their growing collection of pictures and statuary. The drawing-room was subsequently redecorated by Thomas's grandson in the regency style and the house has since remained remarkably unaltered.

Conventionally the hall has a masculine and

Newbridge House

conservative appearance with a strong architectural character that would he entirely at home in any house two decades earlier. Prominent features include a bold modillion cornice wall panelling bold dado rails and skirting boards lugged architraves and a large pedimented chimney-piece incorporating the Cobbe coat of arms. Here in this room guests would have been received and business transacted with tradesmen. To the right lies the dining-room dominated by its original black Kilkenny marble chimney-piece a survival of a post 1765 redecoration of the room which saw a rococo ceiling, plaster wall panels and festoons installed. The Greek key pattern of these panels is reflected in the two Irish Chippendale sideboards which were made especially for the room, above is a magnificent chandelier whose glittering crystal would have been reflected in the elaborate mirror on the wall.

Other rooms in the main building include the library, with its baroque ceiling depicting the four seasons, and the 'Mr Cobbe's Museum or Cabinet of Curiosities' – a curio room dating from 1790 and containing a remarkable display of souvenirs and trophies collected by various members of the family on their numerous travels abroad, particularly in India.

From the museum visitors proceed into the middle hall which forms the north-west corner of the old house. An arch in the end wall guides the eye through a narrow vestibule to the richly modelled pedimented doorcase framing the door of the red drawing-room, which was added by the archbishop's son, Thomas, after 1765. This is a vast room, 42.9 feet by 25.6 feet with a bowed window looking out onto the gardens and an elaborate rococo ceiling and coved cornice by Richard William, a pupil of the great stuccodore Robert West.

The room was redecorated in 1828 and still retains its carpet crimson flock wallpaper and curtains, the latter made by the Dublin firm Mack, Williams and Gibton who also supplied much of the room's furniture. The walls have no less than forty-five pictures, many bought on the advice of the art connoisseur Matthew Pilkington, Vicar of Donabate. Pilkington was a friend of Cobbe's and is best remembered for his spectacular divorce suit with his wife, the amusing and naughty Laetitia, who was described by Virginia Woolf in an essay as 'shady shifting and adventurous'.

The servants' rooms in the basement and yard have also survived intact and have been admirably restored in recent years. The kitchen is fitted with its original screen wall, dresser with jugs and dishes, mid nineteenth-century iron range, whiskey still, duck press, rat traps, numerous copper pots, jelly moulds and wooden tub for salting meat. In the adjacent laundry visitors can inspect a range of equipment used to wash, dry, iron and mend clothes. In the cobbled yard lies the dairy with its marble niches for maturing cheeses, the demesne workers' kitchen, a forge and a carpenter's shop. On display in the coach house is the state carriage made in London in 1790 for 'Black Jack' FitzGibbon, the Lord Chancellor of Ireland and a relation of the Cobbes. The coach was itself black until restored by the National Museum to its former gold magnificence – even the fresco panels had been painted out, probably for the funeral of Queen Victoria.

Located on the western edge of Donabate, 11 miles north of Dublin on the N1.
NGR: O 214501.

COUNTY FERMANAGH

Castle Coole
By the end of the eighteenth century the classicism of Palladio with its Renaissance interpretations of Roman buildings had been replaced by the neo-classical movement proclaiming the primitive virtues, simplicity and tranquil grandeur of Greek architecture. Although Castle Coole still has echoes of Palladianism in its balustraded roof parapets, Venetian windows and centre block with wings, it is without doubt the most perfect neo-classical country house in the British Isles the masterpiece of James Wyatt whose brilliant adoption of earlier designs by Richard Johnson resulted in a monumental, masculine and chaste house enhanced by a gleaming white facade of Portland stone. Its magnificence so impressed the French traveller de Latocraye, when shown around the house in 1797 by its proud new owner, the first Earl of Belmore, that he considered

this 'superb palace' to be too splendid for ordinary mortals, remarking that it was better 'to leave temples to the gods'.

The demesne lands of Castle Coole originally belonged to the Maguires, whose crannog on the lake was abandoned in 1611 when the lands were granted to Roger Atkinson, an English adventurer who built a castle close to the lake shore. The property changed hands a number of times until purchased in 1656 by John Corry, a Belfast merchant of Scottish origin. His son James Corry (1643-1718) replaced the castle in 1709 with a fine Queen Anne house, whose garden layout is still visible 400 yards north west of the present house together with its canal and splendid oak avenue, planted in 1725.

Armar Lowry-Corry (1740-1802) inherited the property through his mother in 1774, determined to build a much grander house to match his considerable wealth, accumulated through three marriages, and his rising status as Baron (1781), viscount (1789) and Earl of Belmore (1797).

Work levelling the site for the new house began in the autumn of 1788, in October 1789 the Dublin architect Richard Johnson submitted plans, and work on the basement commenced. Seven months later, for some unknown reason, Lord Belmore transferred patronage to James Wyatt who adopted Johnson's plan, improved his elevation in 1790 and worked on the house until it was completed in November 1798. Wyatt operated from London and through Alexander Stewart, the clerk of works, he

Castle Coole, Co. Fermanagh

controlled every aspect of the operation, including the internal fittings, the plasterwork and even the design of the furniture. No expense was spared in getting the finest materials and craftsmen available – Portland stone was specially shipped from Dorset for the exterior cladding, and the gangs of imported artificers on site must have seemed like a veritable factory – fourteen joiners, twenty-five stone cutters, twenty-six masons, ten stone sawyers, seventeen carpenters and eighty-three labourers. When completed the cost amounted to £54,000, nearly twice the original estimate, with the result that the first Earl found himself in debt and unable to furnish all of the principal rooms. This task was thus undertaken by his son Somerset, the second Earl (1774-1841), who brought up the leading Dublin upholsterer of the time, John Preston of Henry Street; at a cost of over £17,000, Preston furnished and decorated the rooms 'in a bold and opulent Grecian manner' between 1807 and 1825. In 1817 the second Earl also engaged Sir Richard Morrison to build the impressive stableyard – another project his father had been unable to undertake, though the vaulted tunnel linking the yard to the basement had been completed in 1790.

The sense of proportion, spaciousness and high-quality craftsmanship that visitors will experience in the entrance hall is repeated throughout the house. The room remains much as Wyatt intended except for the recently restored porphyry-red of the walls, which copies a scrape of the colour specified by Preston around 1816. This colour blends well with the screen of red scagliola columns (by the Italian Dominic Bartoli), which support a full Doric entablature running round the room. The bare walls, Portland stone flagging, statues in the wall niches and curtainless windows combine to give the hall a cool, austere, neo-classical feel in striking contrast to the great oval saloon in the middle of the garden front – by far the richest room in the house and one of the most magnificent in Ireland. The ceiling of this room, like the others of the house, was executed by plasterers from the London workshop of Joseph Rose, whom Adam had

Castle Coole

employed for many of his finest décors, including Nostell, Syon and Harewood. The walls are lined with grey scagliola Corinthian pilasters, worked by Bartoli, the capitals for which were sent over from London by Rose. Perhaps the most outstanding features are the magnificent curved mahogany doors which are inlaid with satin wood and hung on pivots. Preston's splendid gilt furniture, mirrors and set of curtains supplied between 1815 and 1821 blend superbly with Wyatt's scheme and give the room a continental Empire atmosphere.

Flanking the saloon are the elegant dining- and drawing-rooms which interconnect to form an enfilade, or cross axis. The decoration of the dining-room seems to have changed little since Wyatt's day and still contains much of the furniture he designed, though the table was supplied by Preston. The drawing-room was entirely furnished and decorated by Preston and has been restored by the National Trust to its regency appearance. The doorcases are richly decorated in pietro duro as they are elsewhere, including the library where splendid bookcases made between 1792 and 1793, by the joiners Peacock and Berry, feature reeded mouldings and ribbon bandings in the uprights, a fluted architrave and guilloche dado. The chimney-piece of statuary marble, carved to simulate festooned drapery, is the finest of six mantels acquired at great expense from Westmacott of London in 1796, while Preston's curtains and valance were replaced in 1857 with the present 'figured crimson silk poplin' supplied by Gibson and Son.

Irish Big Houses

The stone staircase rising from the hall between the library and drawing-room is an adoption of an effective double-flight form used by Wyatt at Heaton. It leads up to a two-storey bedroom lobby – a distinctly Irish feature that is probably a legacy of Johnson's original plan; lit by an oval oculus it is surrounded at attic level by a colonnade inspired by the interior of the Parthenon and the temple of Poseidon at Paestum. Flanking the lobby is the boudoir which was used by the women of the house for sewing, reading, talking and playing the piano. This is an intimate and particularly attractive room whose original early nineteenth-century wall paper, curtains, draperies and valance have been faithfully reproduced by the National Trust in 1980. Opposite lies the sumptuous state bedroom with its magnificent canopied bed and flame silk hangings supplied by Preston in anticipation of a visit by King George IV in 1821. Closed for over four years, this room is happily once again on public view and is one of the wonders of Castle Coole.

The National Trust acquired the house in 1951 and between 1980 and 1991 spent over four million pounds restoring the building and redecorating the interior. Though the present Earl of Belmore and his family still use Castle Coole, their principal residence is an elegant new house sited in the walled garden. It is said that the grey-lag geese, which have been at Castle Coole since 1700, will only go when the Belmores do. Except for some hardship during Hurricane Debbie in 1961, the flock has never shown any desire to leave, and the geese remain a wonderful sight on the lake.

Just SE of Enniskillen on the main Belfast road. NGR: H 260430.

Florence Court
Few country houses can rival the wildly romantic parkland setting of Florence Court or its irresistibly attractive golden-grey façade, whose baroque composition of rustications, balustrades, pedimented niches, lugged surrounds and deep-set quoins has an ethereal, almost bucolic Florence Court quality. The architect and date are unknown, as is so often the case in Ireland, but it was probably built around 1750 for John Cole, Baron Mount Florence, while the flanking arcades and pavilions were completed in 1771 for his son William Cole first Earl of Enniskillen.

The original house at Florence Court was begun around 1718 by Sir John Cole (1680-1726), whose ancestors came from Devonshire during the reign of Queen Elizabeth and lived at Enniskillen Castle until it was burnt in 1710. Cole's 'very costly and sumptuous building', which he named after his wife Florence Wrey, was built in what was then 'a majestic wildness . . . so wild that it was scarce inhabited by any human creatures but ye O's and Mac's, who ranged through the woods like so many freebooters pillaging all that came in their way'.

Florence Court, Co. Fermanagh

The building's early appearance is conjectural, but its basement was evidently retained for the present house, which was erected some time during the 1750s by the first Cole's son, John Cole – the first Lord Mount Florence (1709-67). His tall three-storey seven bay block, which Florence Court appears to have been built in two stages and completed by 1764, has a heavily enriched front facade, while the sides and back are plain by comparison – a characteristic feature of eighteenth century Irish houses. In 1767 work began on the straight arcades and pavilions, which were later completed by William Willoughby

Cole (1736-1803), created Earl of Enniskillen in 1776. These Palladian extensions, attributed to the Sardinian-born architect Davis Ducart, are more refined in detail and execution than the main block and were built as an integral part of a much larger architectural ensemble to the rear, comprising the yards, curved sweeps and crescent lawn. Once completed, the house was given an appropriate Brownian parkland setting between 1778 and 1780 by William King, probably the head gardener at the time, replacing straight tree-lined avenues and other features of a formal layout that had been created in the 1720s.

The vigorous baroque treatment of the exterior is echoed in the large stone flagged hall with its triglyph frieze, handed pilasters, pedimented doorcase, massive Doric sandstone chimney-piece and linen-swag panels. The strong architectural character of this room is repeated in the adjacent library where the walls are lined with finely moulded pinewood bookcases now filled with volumes on loan from Springhill. On the opposite side of the hall lies the service staircase and beyond this the study, whose high coved ceiling is decorated with a rather primitive rococo design of palmettes entwined with swirling scrolls. This room has only recently been opened to the public and contains an important Irish mahogany writing cabinet circa 1730 with a swan-neck pediment and grotesque mask on the frieze.

The large segmental arch at the rear of the hall, which opens onto the magnificent grand staircase, once had a partition wall and double doorcase, but in 1955 this was removed in the mistaken belief that it was a nineteenth-century addition. In fact, this arch was probably blocked around 1760 when the rear of the house was remodelled, as a result of which the staircase hall and its flanking drawing-room and dining-room are quite different in scale and mood from the front of the house. They are bright, large and well proportioned, with splayed windows, simple architraves and vigorous rococo plasterwork in the style of Robert West.

Great panels of swirling foliage decorate the walls of the staircase hall with a Gothick cornice of cusped and ogee arches. Sadly, the elaborate drawing room ceiling was lost in the fire of 1955, but the ceiling in the dining-room survives and is one of the best examples of rococo plasterwork outside of Dublin. It is composed of symmetrically arranged and naturally rendered scrolls of foliage, birds, rocaille work, shells and flamboyant palmiers. The centre-piece is an oval panel containing an eagle Florence Court in high relief representing Zeus, who holds his thunderbolt and hovers in the midst of a stormy empyrean, surrounded by the heads of four cherubs vigorously puffing the winds to the four corners of the earth.

Visitors who look closely at the dining-room ceiling will notice some of the small holes drilled during the 1955 fire to allow the water pumped into the room above to drain away. These holes were the result of quick thinking on the part of the late Duchess of Westminster, Viola Grosvenor, who arrived during the fire to find little urgency about saving family treasures and discovered the old butler on the stairs removing a pair of his master's socks. She managed to get the servants to form a human chain and thus saved much of the house's contents. Unfortunately, the fire destroyed the fine plasterwork of the bedroom landing lantern, the martial decorations of the schoolroom ceiling and the Chinese wallpaper in the red room, while the grand staircase with its wonderful joinery was miraculously only slightly damaged. The plasterwork ceilings in the Venetian room and the entrance hall, which had been completely destroyed, were later expertly restored by the late Sir Albert Richardson.

The National Trust acquired Florence Court as a gift in 1953 from Michael, Viscount Cole (1921-1956), and his father John Henry Cole, fifth Earl of Enniskillen (1876-1963). The contents and most of the land remained in the family and were subsequently inherited by his nephew David Lowry Cole, sixth Earl of Enniskillen (1918-89). The sixth Earl and Countess of Enniskillen left Florence Court for Scotland in January 1974, sadly leaving behind an empty house.

In 1997, Lady Enniskillen re-established contact with the Trust, and gifted back family portraits and other items of Irish memorabilia with strong Florence Court connections. This process continued following her death in 1998 when many more indigenous items were returned to Florence Court, transforming the interiors and reintroducing the gentle atmosphere of the Cole family home. This process continues with additions of indigenous books to the Florence Court library helping to sustain the quintessentially Irish character of this endearing house.

Located 8 miles south west of Enniskillen on the Swanlinbar Road (A4). NGR: H 175343.

COUNTY GALWAY

Kylemore Abbey

Kylemore Abbey is an intensely romantic place, an enchanted fairy-tale castle in the neo-Gothic style that stands dramatically at the foot of a barren mountain in a remote and beautiful part of Connemara – its numerous battlemented and machicolated towers and turrets reflected in the waters of the lake below. For years this amazing house, now a convent, has been the most admired and photographed building in the West of Ireland.

The castle was built between 1863 and 1868 for Mitchell Henry (1826-1911), a highly successful Manchester financier and MP, to the design of James Franklin Fuller and Ussher Roberts, brother of Field Marshal Roberts. The story of its building began in 1852 when Henry was on honeymoon with his bride Margaret Vaughan of Quilly House, County Down. Stopping near Kylemore Pass for an al fresco lunch, the young Mrs Henry looked up and saw a small shooting-box on the opposite hillside, the only dwelling in sight, and exclaimed: 'How I would love

Kylemore Abbey, Co. Galway

to live there.' Ten years later, Mitchell Henry, by now a rich tycoon, purchased the property with its 9,000 acres of moor land, mountain and lake and embarked upon a dream house for his wife.

The building took five years and cost over one and a quarter million pounds – a staggering sum in those days. The completed castle was on a 'Citizen Kane' scale, boasting many splendid reception rooms including a ballroom with a sprung floor, a magnificent staircase, a library, a study and thirty-three bedrooms. There were only four bathrooms, but the house was equipped with a Turkish bath, its water pressure ensured by an elaborate system of hydrants. Mitchell Henry also built a model farm, laundry, dairy, saw mill, ornate chapel and a Gothic church, which was, in part, a replica of Norwich Cathedral. There was a six-acre walled garden and thanks to three miles of hot-water piping, twenty-one greenhouses containing tropical fruit, vineries, peaches, pineries and orangeries. To protect the castle and gardens from constant gales Mitchell Henry planted over three hundred thousand trees. Despite the harsh weather conditions many of these trees grew successfully; examples of which can still be seen by visitors to Kylemore today.

For ten years the Henrys and their nine children lived at Kylemore, entertaining on a lavish scale. Tragedy struck in 1875 when Margaret died on a visit to Egypt. She was buried in a mausoleum at Kylemore, but afterwards her husband could no longer bear to spend much time there. Later his daughter Geraldine was killed when driving a pony and trap locally at Derryinver and shortly afterwards Henry's financial empire started to collapse. In 1902 Kylemore was acquired for a twentieth of its value by Mr Zimmerman, a Chicago businessman, as a present for his daughter who had married the Duke of Manchester. During their tenure from 1902 to 1913, when the estate was mortgaged to money lenders, they made many unfortunate changes, including transforming the lovely ball-room into an enormous kitchen. This conversion was undertaken to satisfy the cook who was expecting to prepare a meal for Edward VII and Queen Alexander on their visit to Connemara in 1903. Their Majesties did, in fact, come – but only for a cup of tea.

The old ballroom is now the chapel of the Irish Dames of Ypres who acquired Kylemore in 1920. This Benedictine congregation was founded originally in 1572 and later established by Dame Lucy Knatchbull at Ypres in 1665. They came to Ireland after their Abbey was destroyed during the Great War and settled at Kylemore, where they established a famous girl's school.

The Abbey, Gothic Church and Mausoleum (where the original owners were laid to rest) are now open to the public. Visitors are also welcome to enjoy the magnificent 6 acre Victorian Walled Garden which has been lovingly restored by the Nuns and which received the Europa Nostra Award in 2002.

Located between Letterfrack and Recess on the N59. NGR: L 74858S.

COUNTY KERRY

Muckross House

Muckross House is best known for its magical parkland setting beside two of Killarney's famous lakes, Lough Leane (the Lower Lake) and Muckross Lake (the Middle Lake). The house is however, worthy of this beautiful location. The great Scottish architect William Burn built it between 1839 and 1843, for

Muckross House, Co. Kerry

Colonel Henry Arthur Herbert and his wife Mary Balfour. At that time, William Burn was just beginning to establish himself as the most influential country house architect of his generation. His brilliance lay principally in his ability to produce comfortable, well-organised houses.

However, Muckross House is also a highly successful example of the Elizabethan Revival style, then very popular in Ireland. It has a great array of tall chimneys, oriels, stepped gables, finials and mullioned windows, that are all skilfully integrated into a crisp, uncluttered composition. This gains much from being

Muckross House

faced with lavish quantities of silvery-pale Portland stone. It is said that this stone was shipped at great expense from Dorset before being hauled, by cart, over the mountains from Kenmare.

A porte cochère, believed to have been added by the Cork architect William Atkins sometime prior to 1861, leads into the entrance hall. The interior was built with the same magnificence of the exterior.

Major Henry Arthur Herbert (Harry) assumed control of the Muckross Estate following his father's death in 1866. Within a few years however, he was experiencing financial difficulties and he spent much of the 1880s and 1890s in America seeking his fortune. Muckross was forfeited to the Standard Life Assurance Company in 1898, when that company foreclosed on the mortgage.

The following year Lord Ardilaun, a member of the Guinness brewing family, purchased the Estate. He sold it in 1910 to William Bowers Bourn, a rich American gold miner. Bourn then presented the house as a wedding present to his daughter Maud and her husband Arthur Vincent. Maud died of pneumonia in 1929.

Three years later her parents and husband bestowed Muckross House, and its 11,000-acre estate, upon the nation. This gift was based on the understanding that its peace and tranquillity would be maintained and that Muckross would become a garden of friendship for the people of Ireland and visitors from abroad.

Muckross House is now managed by a local, voluntary, not-for-profit body, the Trustees of Muckross House (Killarney) Ltd., in conjunction with the National

Irish Big Houses

Parks and Wildlife Service. As well as being the focal point and main visitor attraction within Killarney National Park, Muckross House is also home to the Museum of Kerry Folklife.

The entrance hall is presided over by an impressive set of antlers of the long-extinct Irish elk – an inevitable status symbol of all Irish country houses. From here visitors continue through into the main hall, with its massive oak staircase lit by a window of English crystal. This is a spacious room that serves as a focus for the whole house. It contains an array of stags' heads and three rather ponderous matching sideboards, decorated with some fine woodcarving by the Egan family of Killarney.

In common with most houses of that period, the main hall is flanked by the principal reception rooms, which front the gardens. All have fretted ceilings and immense bay windows, which allow for marvellous views across sweeping lawns to the lake and mountains beyond.

On the north, the dining-room really retains its authentic country house atmosphere. A good mahogany dining-room table, with a set of twelve Chippendale chairs, occupies the centre of the room. The large walnut sideboard was carved in Italy and bears the Herbert crest and family motto 'Every man to his taste'. The window upholstery, fragile and still quite beautiful, is original to this room. It was specially commissioned for the two-night visit of Queen Victoria and Prince Albert, to Muckross, in August 1861.

Passing through the library visitors enter the drawing-room, which overlooks the sunken garden. It features a copy of a portrait of the long-lived Countess of Desmond, a pair of Venetian mirrors and a locally made late nineteenth-century games table inlaid with mother-of-pearl.

Close by visitors may view the suite of rooms occupied by Queen Victoria during her visit. These include the boudoir, the Queen's dressing room and the Queen's bedroom.

On the first floor, off the upper landing, the gentleman's dressing-room, the master bedroom and children's bedroom are next to be admired on the tour of the house. There is also an exhibition of watercolours by the first lady of the house, Mary Balfour Herbert. The main bedroom has a large Sheraton wardrobe and bed, while the pretty children's bedroom contains miniature furniture and toys. The basement still features its old wine cellar, bell corridor, large kitchen and scullery, while other rooms contain the archives of the Muckross Research Library.

The nearby Walled Garden Centre houses the Garden Restaurant, Mucros Craft Shop and three Craft Workshops – Mucros Weaving, Mucros Pottery and Mucros Conservation Bookbindery. Muckross Traditional Farms are also located close by with access directly off the main car park. These working farms portray the life of a local rural townland during the 1930s and 1940s, prior to the introduction of widespread electrification and mechanisation.

Muckross House is located 3 miles south of Killarney on the Kenmare Road. NGR:V 965850.

COUNTY KILDARE

Castletown House

It may justly be said that Castletown is the largest and most splendid country house in Ireland, but it is also arguably the most important for it introduced sophisticated Palladianism from the continent and brought about a revolution in Irish architecture. The building was begun between 1721 and 1722 for William Conolly (1622-1729), the son of a Donegal innkeeper who, through astute dealings in forfeited estates after the Williamite wars, had become the richest man in Ireland. The house is an obvious manifestation of his wealth, but it also reflects the enormous political power that Conolly achieved following his election as Speaker of the Irish House of Commons in 1715 and his appointment as Lord Justice in 1716. Proud of his Irish identity, he consistently used his power to promote Irish interests. It was Conolly who instigated building the Parliament House on College Green, the first of its kind in Europe. Undoubtedly there were similar patriotic and political motivations underlying the building of his house at Castletown.

The design of the house was entrusted to the Florentine Alessandro Galilei (1691-1737), best known for his work on the Lateran Basilica in Rome. Although Galilei returned to Italy in 1719 having spent only a few months in Ireland, work on the building designs did not materialise until a few years later. Building was evidently well underway in July 1722, but with Galilei in Italy it is not clear who was supervising the operation. In 1724, however, the project was taken over by the twenty-five-year-old Edward Lovett Pearce who had just returned from Italy where he was studying the work of Palladio. Pearce had been in close touch with Galilei in Italy (whom he already knew through Vanbrugh, his cousin) and possibly helped him transmit designs back to Conolly in Ireland. Building operations at Castletown continued after Conolly's death in 1729 but came to a halt in 1733 with the early death of Pearce, by now Surveyor General and the most outstanding architect of his generation.

It is not known precisely how much of Castletown is Galilei's work. However, he was certainly responsible for devising the overall scheme of the centre block, which was flanked by colonnades to lower service pavilions in the manner of Palladio's villas in the Veneto – a concept that was completely new in Ireland and later became the prototype and inspiration for numerous houses. The classically correct and regimented main facades of the centre block, both of which are almost identical, have the character of an Italian Renaissance town palazzo and are clearly also Galilei's work; their beauty and serenity are enormously enhanced by the silvery-white limestone which, unlike other Irish lime stones, is free from age-darkening and blackening from the rain. The pavilions, designed by Pearce, are composed of a coarser and less dazzling golden-brown limestone; together with the curved colonnades they have the effect of focussing the eye upon the centre block.

Irish Big Houses

The interior plan of Castletown was probably largely devised by Pearce, although it incorporates some archaic features, such as the arrangement of rooms in an enfilade along the ground-floor garden front. Adhering to the seventeenth-century baroque tradition, these rooms meet in a central saloon and terminate with antechambers at each end. The saloon (now the green drawing-room) opens into the two storey entrance hall, crossed along the inside wall by a corridor running through the central axis of the house. Another corridor directly above this is carried by a balustraded gallery supported by a screen of Ionic columns. It is a magnificent entrance hall – almost certainly designed by Pearce and the only large room that has survived intact from the Speaker's day.

Pearce's device of a columnar screen at one end of the hall was later adopted by many Irish houses, such as Castle Ward in County Down. Another novel feature of the plan which subsequently entered the vocabulary of Irish country house architecture was the location of the main staircase in a separate chamber to the side of the hall. However, this chamber evidently remained without its staircase for forty years, as Speaker Conolly's widow preferred to leave the interior unfinished though she continued to live at Castletown in great style until her death in 1752. She was, none-the-less, responsible for building work in the demesne, notably the Conolly Folly (1740), the Wonderful Barn (1743) and the Batty Langley Lodge (circa 1745).

Castletown's interior was largely created during the time of Tom Conolly, the Speaker's great nephew, who inherited the property in 1758 when he was twenty-four. That same year he married the fifteen-year-old Lady Louisa Lennox, daughter of the second Duke of Richmond, whose older sister Emily had already married James, the Earl of Kildare, and was living nearby at Carton. By all accounts Tom Conolly had a weak, indecisive character, but Louisa was extremely dynamic and immediately set about completing the house.

The staircase hall was Louisa's first objective. She employed the Dutch-Italian sculptor and stonemason Simon Vierpyl to install the magnificent Portland-stone cantilevered staircase in 1760; the unusual brass balustrade in the form of Doric columns is signed 'A. King Dublin 1760'. As substantial payments were made to the famous Swiss-Italian stuccodores – the Francini brothers – in 1765 it may be assumed that the plasterwork in the staircase hall was applied then, except for the cornice and coffered ceiling which belong to Pearce's time. The Francini brothers first came to Ireland in l739 and are credited with the introduction of human figures into plaster decoration; characteristically, their plasterwork on the staircase incorporates a number of family portraits as well as large canvases, notably The Boar Hunt thought to be by Flemish artist Paul de Vos.

Alterations and improvements to the house during the period of 1760 to 1766 included the creation of the dining-room and work on the red and green drawing rooms. On stylistic grounds it has been maintained

Irish Big Houses

that these rooms, which feature ceilings of Jonesian-inspired geometrical plasterwork, were designed by Sir William Chambers – an argument supported by the fact that Simon Vierpyl was one of his proteges and may have supervised the work since Chambers never actually came to Ireland.

The dining-room to the left of the hall was created by throwing together two earlier rooms, while at the same time the ground-floor windows were lowered twenty-one inches. It was in the dining-room that legend has it Tom Conolly entertained the devil, whom he had met out hunting and invited back, believing him to be a 'dark stranger' but realising the truth after his guest had removed his boots to reveal hairy feet shaped like cloven hooves. A priest was summoned in haste, he hurled his breviary at the devil missed and cracked a mirror, whereupon the devil took fright and vanished up the chimney, leaving behind a split hearthstone and a cracked mirror to this day.

The red drawing-room contains a japanned lacquer cabinet that belonged to old Mrs Conolly and is inscribed 'Mrs Conolly to Miss Burten' with drawers painted with charming Italianate scenes. The green drawing-room, formerly the saloon, has been restored with green silk copied from the original fabric (1765) and gilded fillet copied from Chamber's design for the fillet in the gallery at Osterley Park. Flanking the door are portraits of Speaker Conolly and his wife Katherine by Jervas. The adjacent print room was created by Lady Louisa Conolly between 1766 and 1768 with the help of her sister Sarah. The fashion for pasting engravings and mezzo tints onto walls during the long winter days became very popular at that time. The print room at Castletown is possibly the earliest to survive – it is certainly the only one that still exists in Ireland.

Apparently inspired by her success in the print room, Louisa Conolly decided to redecorate the long gallery – an eighty-foot-long room on the first floor directly above the garden front enfilade. She had the old plaster panels 'knocked off smack smooth' and Pompeian decoration painted onto the walls by two English artists, Charles Reuban Riley and Thomas Riley, between 1775 and 1777. Plans to remove the old Pearce ceiling and frieze were dropped and the ceiling was instead redecorated with colours matching the walls. The glass chandeliers from Murano near Venice were bought to match the room's colour, though Louisa was disappointed when they arrived, claiming they were the wrong blue.

Four doors once led into the room but after remodelling there was only one entrance, although another blind door had been created to disguise the fact that the landing entrance was placed off centre. The lunette above the doors is copied from Guido Reni's Aurora, while a reproduction portrait of Tom Conolly hangs over the mantelpiece at the end of the room. The original was painted in 1758 by Mengs in Rome and is now in the collections of the National Gallery of Ireland. A visitor in 1778 found the room furnished 'in the most delightful manner with fine glasses, books, musical instruments, billiard table – in short, everything that you can think of . . . and though so large it is so well fitted that it is the warmest, most comfortable looking place I ever saw and they tell me they live in it quite in the winter, for the servants can bring in dinners at one end without anyone hearing at the other.'

Tom Conolly died in 1803 but Lady Louisa lived on for many years. She eventually died in 1821, seated in a tent erected on the lawn in front of Castletown, for it was her wish that she should go looking at the house she had loved so much. The house then passed to the grandson of Tom Conolly's sister Harriett, Colonel Edward Michael Pakenham, who changed his name to Conolly. He was succeeded in 1848 by his son Thomas Conolly (1823-76), and later in turn by both of his sons. Upon the death of Major Conolly in 1956, Castletown was inherited by Lord Carew who put it up for auction in 1965.

The land was bought by property speculators who proceeded to build a housing estate beside the 250-year-old lime avenue. Ultimately in 1967 the decaying house and 120 acres were bought in the eleventh hour by Desmond Guinness in order to save Castletown for posterity. It became the headquarters of the Irish Georgian Society, who with the help of weekend volunteers and money raised at home and abroad managed to repair the building and refurnish some of the rooms. In 1994 it was acquired by the Office of Public Works and its future is now finally assured, although the battle to recover its dispersed contents may be waged for generations to come.

Located 1 mile north east of Celbridge. NGR: N 980342.

COUNTY LAOIS

Emo Court

The spectacular mansion of Emo Court, with its fine garden and parkland setting, is perhaps best known as James Gandon's sole venture into the field of monumental domestic architecture. It was designed around 1790 on the same magnificent scale as his Custom House (1781-91) and Four Courts (1786) and in common with these was built in the neo-classical style the style in which Gandon had established himself as the pre-eminent architect of late eighteenth-century Ireland.

The house was commissioned by John Dawson Viscount Carlow and the first Earl of Portarlington man of undoubted architectural knowledge who was instrumental in bringing Gandon to Ireland. Daws engaged Gandon primarily to design the nearby church at Coolbanagher (1782-83); later he requested plans for a new county seat to replace Dawson Court, built by his grandfather Ephraim Dawson in the early eighteenth century. A new site was chosen for the house which was named Emo – an Italianised version of Imoe the original Irish name of the demesne. As designed by Gandon, it has a giant pedimented Ionic portico dominating the centre of the entrance front, flanked by two end pavilions making it in all a nine-bay composition with two storeys over a basement. Panels

Emo Court, Co. Laois

containing Coadstone reliefs of putti representing the Arts and a pastoral scene, dated 1794, crown the blind attics of the pavilions.

Sadly, Gandon's building was never completed as Lord Portarlington died of an illness when out campaigning during the 1798 rebellion. Despite their motto 'Virtue is the Way of Life', the family fortune was subsequently dissipated through gambling and the second Earl was unable to finance further building until 1834 when he employed the English architect Lewis Vulliamy, assisted by Arthur and John Williamson of Dublin, to make improvements.

They worked on the interior as well as completing the garden front giving it a portico of four tall Ionic columns with a balustraded entablature to complement Gandon's front elevation. Finally in 1861, after the Encumbered Estates Court came close to ordering a compulsory sale of the estate, the third Earl somehow found enough money to build the great rotunda, whose copper-clad dome rising from behind the garden front was designed by William Caldbeck of Dublin. The mile-long Wellingtonia avenue was planted at this time and formal gardens laid out around the house.

The Portarlingtons sold Emo in 1930 to the Society of Jesus for use as a seminary. In 1969 the property was bought from the Jesuits by C. D. Cholmeley-Harrison of Woodstown House in County Waterford, who has subsequently carried out a magnificent restoration and refurbishment of the house upon the advice of the late Sir Albert Richardson's firm, a renowned specialist In the conservation of Georgian buildings.

Unfortunately, much of Gandon's interior at Emo failed to survive nineteenth-century alterations An important exception is the entrance hall – an attractive single-storey room whose apsidal ends were painted with trompe l'oeil paintings in the 1970s to-represent plaster decoration that Gandon had originally intended. The hall leads directly into Calbeck's great rotunda – a magnificent circular space lit by a lantern in a high coffered dome which rests on Siena-marble pilasters with richly gilded Corinthian capitals. A more successful room would be difficult to find in Ireland, except perhaps for Johnson's amazing staircase rotunda at Townley Hall.

The rotunda is flanked by the dining-room on one side and the library, formerly the anteroom, on the other. Both rooms have handsome plasterwork ceilings designed by Vulliamy – that in the library has gold painted rococo decoration which matches the room's remarkable chimney-piece, an enormous white marble monstrosity packed with playful putti and an excess of grapes. From the present library the visitor enters the old library, now the drawing-room – an enormous room that extends the entire way down from the front to the back of the house. It is divided by screens of Connemara marble columns, has distempered apple green walls and extends into a wide curving bow in the centre of one of the long sides. Some fine pictures hang in this room, notably a large canvas of Christ and the Woman of Samaria at the Well by Francesco Trevisani, together with paintings by Abraham Bisschop, Lemaire Poussin and the Irishman James Arthur O'Connor. There is also a fine mid eighteenth-century Irish mahogany settee and a good collection of ceramics including a delicately adorned little Meissen tray.

The restoration of Emo did not end with the house. Mr Cholmeley-Harrison has also admirably restored the gardens, planting many new trees and shrubs. In an area of the demesne park now owned by the Forest Commission stands the ruin of a building known as the Temple – a remarkable gazebo built around 1760 on alignment with Dawson's Court. It consists of a triumphal arch surmounted by an octagonal two-storied turret that was formerly domed. No doubt it was used for entertaining as it had a kitchen in the basement. A short distance away on Spike Hill is an obelisk.

6 miles south of Portlaoise. NGR: N 539066.

COUNTY LONDONDERRY

Springhill

Considering the harsh and unappealing conditions that still prevailed in late seventeenth-century Ulster, it is perhaps surprising that country seats developing at that time were often pleasant and unassuming buildings exuding a feeling of warmth. Sadly, such houses from this period are now rare, though one particularly attractive and well-preserved example is Springhill – a charming and almost timeless building whose white washed front facade still brings to mind 'something of the ancient dignity of resident landlords' as it did for Sampson, writing nearly two centuries ago.

The early history of Springhill is a little elusive, but the present house was built by William 'Good-Will' Conyngham as part of his marriage contract to Anne Upton in 1680 to 'erect a convenient dwelling house of lime and stone, two stories high, with necessary office houses, gardens and orchards'. It is not known if a dwelling stood here previously, but the townland of Ballindrum (Springhill) had been bought for £200 by Good-Will Conyngham's father in 1658. Earlier it belonged to a London company, the Salters, and prior to this had formed part of the ancient territory of the O'Cahan's.

Although enlarged with wide canted-bay pavilions in the late eighteenth-century, the house that Good-Will built survives much as he left it – a gable-ended block of two storeys over a basement with a steeply pitched roof, solid brick chimneys at each end and tall,

Springhill, Co. Londonderry

thin windows in a seven-bay symmetrical front façade. Springhill faces north onto a deep courtyard flanked by long, low office ranges with pointed windows (a later insertion) and curvilinear 'Holborn gables' – a Flemish type which seems to have been much used in late seventeenth-century Ulster. Front courtyards were a standard feature of the period and Springhill was originally entered from the north through large gates aligned upon a long, straight avenue. The main out buildings, grouped around a series of small yards flanking the house, include a recently restored barn with pistol loops and an important oak roof, which like that of the main house incorporated butt purloins, rare in Ireland. Tree-ring dating by Queen's University, Belfast, revealed a date of 1694 for a lintel from this barn, while a floor joist timber from the attic of the main house produced a felling date of 1697.

The seventeenth-century building has a tripartite plan with a centrally placed stair projection at the back. Approached by four stone steps leading to a door with a plain stone frame, it reveals a square entrance hall with bold bolection plaster panelling that is probably contemporary with the house. The door to the staircase hall is flanked by two pikes used in the Battle of Vinegar Hill, County Wexford, during the 1798 rebellion.

This magnificent broad staircase is the real glory of Springhill and one of the earliest to survive in Ireland. The treads are made of oak while the handrail and balusters – alternately plain and spiral twisted are made from yew. Ancestral portraits line the walls above, including one of Good-Will Conyngham, while at the foot of the stairs is a heavy oak chest inscribed 'John Smith maid this in 1714'.

To the left of the entrance hall lies the gun room, a dark, masculine room which retains its original bolection moulded oak panelling. Formerly the dining-room, it must have been made into a small drawing-room around 1770 as restoration work during the 1960s accidentally revealed pretty handprinted English wall paper in the panel frames. Later it became home to a fine collection of guns and swords reflecting the family's military past. Among the items on display are a few bulky blunderbusses, a Kentucky rifle, duelling pistols and a number of flintlocks, later converted to muzzleloaders and used in the siege of Derry in 1689.

The library on the opposite side of the hall houses an outstanding collection of books, most of which were acquired by Colonel William Conyngham (1723-84). Opposite the fireplace is a fine library cabinet whose double-arched top dates from the late seventeenth century, while a fascinating medicine chest full of drawers and bottles stands beside the drawing-room door; originally belonging to the Duke of Marlborough, he gave it to his aide-de-camp, the third viscount Molesworth, after he saved his life during the Battle of Ramillies in 1706. The set of heavy chairs in the room are early nineteenth-century copies of Jacobean originals; according to family history, the original chairs were destroyed by Olivia, second wife of George Lennox-Conyngham (1752-1816). One chair was spared, however, and Maxwell, the estate carpenter, remade the lot.

The large and lofty drawing-room, added by Colonel William Conyngham sometime after he inherited the property in 1765, creates a striking contrast to the small rooms of the original house. French Empire sofas, Louis XV tables and an armchair, a Dutch rosewood cabinet and a circular mahogany inlaid regency table grace the scene, while family portraits by Hugh Douglas Hamilton, William Hoare and Pompeo Batoni hang on the walls. There is also a pretty portrait of Harriet Molesworth by Sir Francis

Irish Big Houses

Cotes. The unfortunate Harriet lost her leg while trying to escape a fire at her London home, and an ivory walking stick presented to her by King George III is displayed on a small Chinese cupboard beneath her portrait.

Next to the drawing-room and overlooking the park is the dining-room, added by William, 'Wims', Lenox Conyngham (1792-1858) shortly after his marriage in 1819. It has red flock wallpaper, a set of marquetry walnut fiddle-back chairs of the William and Mary period (circa 1700) and a chimney-piece of yellow marble brought from Herculaneum by the eccentric Earl Bishop of Derry and presented by him to the family in the early 1780s. Over the chimney-piece hangs a still life of birds in the manner of Hondecoeter and on the opposite wall is the celebrated picture known as The Grand Tour Group, painted in Rome between 1772 and 1773 and attributed to John Brown. It depicts John Staples with Thomas Orde, Richard Neville, Sir William Young and James Byres admiring an antique sculpture. The picture is appropriately flanked by portraits of John Staples's daughter Charlotte and her husband Wims Lenox-Conyngham.

Elsewhere in Springhill are many small rooms, old powder closets and even a secret staircase now permanently concealed. There are curious sloping alcoves for beds in the attics and below, on the first floor, a charming day nursery. One of the two bedrooms open to the public is the blue room where George Lenox Conyngham shot himself in 1816 after spending many months 'in a melancholy state of mind'. His wife, Olivia, haunts the scene; her ghost is one of the most widely authenticated phantoms in Ulster.

Outside, in the old laundry yard, lies an important costume collection begun in 1964 with a loan from the Pack-Beresford family and subsequently expanded by the National Trust. It now contains over 2,300 items, including a Court Mantua made in England in 1759 and featuring brocaded Spitalfields silk. The collection is displayed in rotation each year.

Springhill was given as a gift to the National Trust in 1957 by Captain William Lenox-Conyngham shortly before his death. Included in the transfer was the magnificent 300-year-old beech avenue which sadly had to be replanted in 1984 after the trees developed beech bark disease.

Located near Moneymore on the Coagh Road (B18). NGR: H 869828.

COUNTY LOUTH

Beaulieu

On the banks of the River Boyne, lying a few miles upstream from Drogheda, stands Beaulieu, alias Bewley – a house of considerable charm and enormous architectural importance. It was built in the years of peace and prosperity following the Restoration in 1660, when Irish landowners abandoned their medieval castles and built unfortified luxurious seats. Almost all known examples of these Carolinian country

Beaulieu, Co. Louth

houses have now vanished and only the unchanged splendour and refinement of Beaulieu survives to bear witness to this major turning point in the development of Irish architecture.

The house was built between 1661 and 1667 by Sir William Tichborne, who had been granted possession of the property by Charles II in 1662. His father, Sir Henry Tichborne, the prominent military commander in the Civil War, had resided as a tenant in the old castle at Beaulieu since 1650, having purchased the rights from the mortgages – the Peppard brothers. From the thirteenth century, ownership of the castle, which stood north west of the present house, had belonged to the Plunkett family, but in 1639 it was mortgaged and in 1642 was forfeited by the Cromwellian regime in retaliation for William Plunkett's participation in the 1641 rebellion.

Externally the house has remained virtually unaltered since the 1660s, although until the nineteenth century it was surrounded by a twelve-foot-high protective hedge. Beaulieu is a seven-bay two-storied building and like many English houses of that time was built in the so-called 'artisan mannerist' style, with cantilevered eaves carried on a massive wooden modillion course and a dormered attic in a high-hipped roof surmounted by tall, symmetrical chimney stacks. The rendered walls are of stone, but delicately rubbed orange-pink bricks from Holland have been used for the window surrounds and the string coursing which firmly encloses the house. Any sense of monotony is broken by the grouping of windows on the side façades and by the pushing forward of the two end bays of the front elevation.

The interior still contains a great deal of its original fittings. The lofty two-storied hall, lit by first-floor windows, retains its arched doorways, cornice and large chimney-piece and overmantel, the latter adorned with a painting of the town of Drogheda. Both the dining-room and drawing-room have kept their red pine panelling with bolection mouldings (a form of moulding which projects in front of the face of the frame) and their original ceilings with central ovals surrounded by heavy floral garlands. The ceiling in the drawing-room features a skewed-perspective painting attributed to Willem van der Hagen depicting a gallery opening into a clouded and cherubined sky.

Most of the subsequent alterations to the interior were undertaken in the early eighteenth century by the son of the builder of the house, Sir Henry Tichborne, the first and last Baron Ferrard (1663-1731) who succeeded to the property in 1693. His most important addition was the grand staircase with its finely carved balusters and ramps at the newels, installed between 1722 and 1723. Other alterations at this time included a corridor on the first-floor landing and elaborate woodcarvings added to the arches over the doors in the front hall. It is also likely that Tichborne was responsible for replacing the original mullioned and casement windows with their sash openings.

After Lord Ferrard's death from apoplexy in 1731 the house was inherited by his son-in-law, William Aston, MP; after 1769 it passed to William Aston's brother-in-law, Thomas Tipping, MP, from whom it devolved through the female line to the Montgomery family where transferring through four male descendants to Mrs Sidney Waddington (nee Montgomery) until 2005 when her daughter Mrs Gabriel Defreitas inherited. This remarkable house has thus remained in the same family for nine generations, covering a period of over 350 years.

Located a few miles from Drogheda on the banks of the Boyne between the Baltray and Termonfeckin roads. NGR: O 128767.

COUNTY MAYO

Westport House

Designed by the famous architects Richard Cassels and James Wyatt, Westport House is the largest and most important 18th-century country house west of the Shannon. The house was built and is still privately owned by the Browne Family. It is one of the few remaining historic homes in Ireland still complete with a large amount of the original contents. Since first opening to the public in 1960 visitors have marvelled at the building's quality and contents and, above all, its magnificent setting on the edge of Clew Bay.

Westport House is the work of several architects, although the main mass of the building was designed in 1730 by Richard Cassels for John Browne, later the first Earl of Altamont (1709-76). The house was built on the foundations of a castle which had formerly belonged to the 16th-century Pirate Queen, Grace O'Malley. The castle had been acquired and much enlarged by the first Earl's grandfather, Colonel John Browne (1636-1711) who had married Grace O'Malley's great-great granddaughter, Maude Burke. He was a Jacobite who lost his fortune after the Williamite victory at the Boyne. In reduced circumstances, the family moved to Mount Browne outside Westport, but their fortune prospered again when John Browne (Colonel John Browne's grandson) married Anne Gore, sister of the Earl of Aran in 1729.

The Cassel's east front of the house as it is today, with its nine-bay façade was built with the finest

Westport House, Co. Mayo

limestone taken from the quarry south of the estate farmyard and was executed by local craftsmen. The front hall entrance has a magnificent barrel-vaulted ceiling. Its tripartite doorway, approached by a lengthy flight of steps, has a wide pediment supported by three satyrs' masks. In the centre of these are the Arms of the Earl of Altamont, which must have been added after 1771. Above there are roundels for busts, a three-windowed attic and two-winged eagles of the family crest at either end of the cornice.

We can see how Westport looked in 1761 from two landscapes by George Moore hanging on the stairs. They show the house in a parkland setting with young plantations, bridges, salmon leaps and the sea coming right up to the house walls. The paintings were commissioned on the completion of John Browne's new park – a massive undertaking that involved not just landscaping and planting trees, but moving the town of Westport from its original position around the house to its present location about a mile distant, where a new planned town was created.

Cassel's house extended round three sides of an inner court, but between 1776 and 1778 its size was enormously increased when a fourth side was built to the designs of the Cork-born architect Thomas Ivory. This was commissioned by the second Earl of Altamont – Peter –whose marriage to an heiress of sugar plantations in Jamaica had made him one of Ireland's wealthiest men. After his death in 1780 the third Earl, John Denis (1756-1809), who was made Marquess of Sligo in 1800, employed James Wyatt to complete the interior. Wyatt's original drawings, dated 1781, are on view in the house. More rooms were added at basement level in 1816 when large terraces were built on either side of the house by the second Marquess, Howe Peter (1788-1845) – remembered for his friendships with George IV and Lord Byron. He brought back to Westport the two columns from the doorway of the Treasury of Atreus at Mycenae when touring Greece in 1812. They remained forgotten in the cellars until discovered by the sixth Marquis who presented them to the British Museum on 1906 on condition that they supply him with the replicas now standing on the south front of the house.

The entrance hall is the only surviving interior by Cassels that still remains intact. It has a Doric frieze and a magnificent coffered barrel-vaulted ceiling that has been compared to the roof of the temple of Aesculapius at Spoleto. Light pours into the room through a delicately wrought brass lunette above the frieze, though at one time there was also a Venetian window at the west end. In 1960 the tenth Marquess of Sligo – Denis Edward removed the original monumental black marble chimney-piece, typical of Cassels, and replaced it with a George III Carrara marble one which was brought from Welbeck Abbey in Nottinghamshire.

The brilliant Waterford Chandelier in the Front Hall is one of several in the house. In 1858 the third Marquess of Sligo – George commissioned the parquet floors in the house. He also installed the imperial staircase which replaced Howe Peter's (his father's) library where originally the open courtyard had been. Approached through arches from the hall, this grand staircase of Sicilian marble was designed by George Wilkinson to replace two smaller ones on either side. The cantilevered stairs have undercut treads, while the metalwork balustrade, which was made by Skidmore of Coventry, has eagle motifs that were once gilded. In a recess on the half-landing is CT Fuller's marble Angel of Welcome. Close by are several delightful local landscapes by James O'Connor and a pair of large chalk drawings of six of Howe Peter's (the second Marquess's) children by Frank W. Wilkins.

The library to the left of the hall replaces one that was designed by Wyatt's son Benjamin in 1819 and subsequently destroyed by fire in 1826. It is a comfortable room whose walls are lined with bookcases stretching to within two feet of the ceiling; to the right of the door is a secret passage said to have been used to hide arms. On the other side of the hall lies the drawing-room, now used as a dining area for special events. This has a frieze of Etruscan figures and a sky painted ceiling circa 1825, as well as a very fine marble mantelpiece by John Flaxman. The adjoining long gallery, where there is a collection of family portraits was originally decorated by James Wyatt in 1781. It was later remodelled by his son Benjamin, who had a more minimalist approach and removed all the plasterwork decorations.

Although Wyatt never actually came to Ireland, let alone Westport, the delicate Adam-style plasterwork in the dining-room must rank among the best examples of his work. Both walls and ceilings incorporate medallions of classical figures with garlands, bows, festoons and gilded ears of wheat. Originally coloured green and white, the room was repainted grey, blue and gold with touches of red in 1915. The mahogany doors came from the family estates in Jamaica, while the massive sideboards supported by the family eagles were made by Gillow's for Howe Peter – the second Marquess. Also on display in this room are Colonel John Browne's dinner service, Waterford glass finger bowls, eighteenth-century silver dish rings and a potato bowl of bog oak and silver that has

Irish Big Houses

belonged to the family since the seventeenth century.

There are more family heirlooms in the small dining room, most notably Mayo Legion Flag which was brought to Ireland by General Humbert when he landed in Killala in 1798 with French troops. Elsewhere in the house visitors can see the exceptionally beautiful ceiling by Thomas Ivory above the oak staircase, the Wyatt mantelpiece in the morning room and the Chinese room with its beautifully handpainted eighteenth-century wallpaper, which tells the same story as the willow pattern plate.

The Westport House Estate presently belongs to the eleventh Marquess and Marchioness of Sligo – Jennifer and Jeremy. The house first opened in 1960 to visitors and is still open during the season. Many outdoor family adventure activities have been added over the years. There is also a camping and caravan park on the grounds – all in the cause of trying to save a magnificent piece of history and heritage.

Located just outside the town of Westport. NGR: L 987852.

COUNTY ROSCOMMON

Clonalis House

Whatever the great Victorian mansion at Clonalis may lack in architectural beauty, it certainly gains through its historical associations with the O'Connor Dons, descendants of the last High Kings of Ireland whose possession of these lands can be traced back over 1,500 years. The ruins of the old ancestral seat – an attractive late seventeenth-century gable-ended house incorporating a medieval castle – can still be seen in the demesne. This was abandoned in 1880 after the completion of the present house, a large, rather grim cement-rendered building of two storeys with a basement and dormered attic. Its peculiar mixture of Queen Ann Revival and Victorian Italianate styles is typical of the work of its designer – Frederick Pepys Cockerell, a young and popular English architect who died shortly after building work at Clonalis had begun in 1879.

On the lawn in front of the house stands the inauguration stone of the O'Connors, originally erected at Carnfree, the ancient seat of the High Kings of Connaught some nine miles distant. The main entrance to the house is through a balustraded porch set at the base of a projecting Italianate tower. Entering the building, visitors will be struck by the height of the hall, whose modillion ceiling cornice is supported by graceful arches and Ionic columns of pink marble from Mallow. The room has a striking marble bolection chimney-piece, while behind an

Irish Big Houses

arcade stands a fine staircase with an oak handrail and pitch-pine balusters. Over the stairs hangs a banner which was carried by Denis O'Connor Don at the coronation of George V in 1911 – the first Irish Gaelic family to be so honoured. Family portraits here include Hugh O'Connor, who founded Tucson in Arizona, and Major Owen of Ballintubber who lost his lands under Cromwell, regained them under Charles II and mortgaged them to raise troops for James II.

A broad arched corridor leads from one side of the hall to the main reception rooms. The first of these to be entered is the large and rather charming drawing-room, which has fine Boulle furniture and some beautifully modelled figures of Meissen, Limoges and Minton porcelain. In the library mahogany bookcases hold over 5,000 books, including the diaries of Charles O'Connor of Belnagare (1710-90), the great historian and antiquary. There are also facsimiles of many early illuminated Irish manuscripts and over 100,000 letters and documents. The room's marble chimney-piece is flanked by niches for turf, as is the chimney in the dining room where the furniture is mostly Irish Sheraton and the dinner service Mason ironstone. The Roman Catholic chapel contains a number of relics from penal times, including the altar from a secret chapel located in the outbuildings of the old house and a chalice once used by Bishop O'Rourke to celebrate mass, which unscrews into separate pieces for easy concealment.

Some of the most interesting items in the house are found in the billiard room, now converted into a small museum. Here visitors can peruse letters and papers from the family archives, including notes written by such famous personalities as O'Connell, Parnell, Gladstone, Trollope, Napper Tandy, Samuel Johnson and Laurence Stern. However, pride of place in this room is the harp that was once played by Turlough Carolan (1670-1738), the famous blind musician and last of the traditional Irish bards. He often played at Clonalis and once remarked that 'when I am among the O'Connors, the harp has the old sound in it'.

Located 6 miles west of Castlerea on the N60. NGR: M 6608143.

Strokestown Park House
Members of the Irish nobility sometimes had rather grand notions, and so it was at Strokestown where the second Lord Hartland laid out a street he wanted wider than the Ringstrasse in Vienna. At one end of this tree lined mall lies a magnificent Gothic arch that leads to Strokestown Park House, one of Ireland's finest Palladian houses and seat of the Pakenham Mahon family from 1660 to 1979. It now belongs to James Callery of Westward Garage, who purchased the property complete with its contents, saving it from almost certain demolition. He has subsequently carried out a major restoration programme and opened it to the public.

From the front, the house looks enormous with its central block linked by curved quadrants to wings that are prolonged by screen walls with niches and

Strokestown Park House, Co. Roscommon

pedimented archways. The main house has seven bays with three storeys over a basement and seems largely to date from 1696 – the date carved on a stone by the front door. The top storey and balustrade were added later probably around 1740 when the architect Richard Castle built the wings for Thomas Mahon (1701-82) MP for Roscommon for forty-two years.

His son Maurice, who became Baron Hartland upon accepting a Union peerage in 1800, made further additions and modifications to the house, including the inlaid mahogany doors, chimney-pieces and cornices as well as the library. In 1819 Lieutenant

Strokestown Park House

General Thomas Mahon second Lord Hartland, employed the architect J. Lynn to carry out some more improvements, such as the addition of the porch and giant pilasters to the front. Except for the gardens, few changes were later carried out at Strokestown and it remained the centre of a vast 30,000-acre estate until the present century.

In contrast to the external grandeur of the house, the interior is quite intimate, with surprisingly small rooms – a product of the early date of much of the building. Early eighteenth-century wood panelling survives in parts of the house, notably in the main staircase hall, but many rooms were redecorated in regency times, such as the dining-room which still has its early nineteenth-century furniture, including a bath-size turf bucket and wonderful pinkish-red damask wallpaper. Regency additions to the house incorporated the study, which also retains its original furnishings, and the smoking room which was converted into a laboratory and photographic dark-room by Henry Pakenham-Mahon, an amateur scientist, in the 1890s. The finest regency addition to the house was the library at the back; originally built as a ball-room with a bowed wall at one end to accommodate musicians. This well-proportioned room has an exuberant and welcoming atmosphere that is remarkable for its unique Chippendale bookcases and for the beauty of its brown and gold wallpaper, made especially for these walls in the early nineteenth century.

The old kitchen in the left wing of the house is approached from the dining-room along a curved corridor, past store rooms for kitchen utensils and sporting equipment. Fitted with spits and ovens for baking, roasting and smoking, this kitchen has its original balustraded gallery which crosses the high ceilinged room lengthwise – the only example of its kind to survive in Ireland. Once a familiar feature of many Irish eighteenth-century houses, especially those designed by Richard Castle, these galleries allowed the housekeeper to supervise affairs below – one tradition at Strokestown relates that menus were dropped from the balcony on Monday mornings with the instructions to the cook for the week's meals.

The wing to the right of the central block contains magnificent vaulted stables carried on Tuscan columns – very similar to stables that Castle built for Carton (l739) and Russborough (1741). An underground passage linked these stables to the yard on the north side of the house. The estate office was also housed in this wing – a surprising location, for it meant that the tenantry had to come here rather than to an office in the village to pay their rent. The family's relationship with their tenantry during part of the nineteenth century was not always good.

Major Denis Mahon, who succeeded to Strokestown on the death of the third and last Lord Hartland in 1845, was so unpopular a landlord during the famine years that he was shot whilst returning from a meeting of the Roscommon Relief Committee in 1847, apparently on suspicion of having chartered unseaworthy ships to transport emigrants from his estate to America. His successors were much better regarded and his great-granddaughter and last owner, Mrs Olive Hales-Pakenham-Mahon, was a much loved figure in this part of Ireland. She died in 1981, leaving a house filled with the trappings of three centuries of unbroken family occupation.

Located 10 miles west of Longford on the Dublin to Ballina Road (N5).
NGR: M 937808.

COUNTY SLIGO

Lissadell House

Few houses have such colourful associations as Lissadell – the large and austere Grecian Revival home of the Gore-Booth family, beautifully situated amidst woods and glades on the north shore of Sligo Bay and immortalised by William Butler Yeats in his poem 'In Memory of Eva Gore-Booth and Con Markiewicz'. As a young man Yeats spent many happy days here with Eva, whom he likened to a gazelle, and Constance, the 'acknowledged beauty of the county'. In later years he fondly remembered the lofty bright rooms of Lissadell with their 'great windows open to the south' and the 'great sitting room as high as a church and all things in good taste'.

Even fewer Georgian houses have been so meticulously restored as Lissadell in the few short years since it was acquired from the Gore Booth family in 2004 by Edward Walsh and Constance Cassidy. As well as being a home to their young family

Lissadell House, Co. Sligo

of seven children, Lissadell is a showcase of Georgian architecture and a thriving horticultural estate. The house and gardens are open to the public all year round.

The Lissadell Estate had fallen into decline after the death of Josslyn Gore Booth in 1944. Indeed, writing about Lissadell for the *Sunday Times* around forty years ago, the BBC's Anne Robinson ('The Weakest Link') observed that 'the garden is overgrown, the greenhouses are shattered and empty, the stables beyond repair, the roof of the main block leaks badly and the paintings show patches of mildew'. Now, however the grandeur of the old rooms and furnishing of Lissadell have been restored, and remain steeped in remembrance of the many remarkable people who have lived here.

The Gore-Booths stem from an Elizabethan soldier settler, Sir Paul Gore, ancestor of the Earls of Arran. The Sligo branch first settled at nearby Ardtermon Castle (now restored) but in the eighteenth century moved to a house near the shore at Lissadell. Unfortunately, the damp situation and the danger from high tides was always a problem, so in 1833 Sir Robert Gore-Booth, fourth Bart (1805-76), commissioned the experienced Manchester architect Francis Goodwin (1784-1835) to design the present house. The conservative tastes of both patron and architect resulted in the adoption of a chaste neo-classical design – the last time this style was used for a large country house in Ireland. The exterior walls of grey Ballysodare limestone incorporate very little ornament apart from corner pilasters and a strong horizontal frieze, while the treatment of the interior is similarly austere, though relieved by a wonderful sensation of bright light and space pervading the rooms.

A porte cochère with big oak doors gives access to a broad flight of steps leading up to the front hall – a lofty two-storey room with square Doric columns below and Ionic columns above. Kilkenny marble is used for the floor and also for the magnificent double staircase, notable for its iron balusters decorated with winged birds. Beyond the hall in the core of the house lies an enormous apse-ended gallery sixty-five-feet long lit by skylights and a clerestory with tall Doric pilasters along one side and freestanding Ionic columns along the other. It was once the music room and retains its original Gothic chamber organ pumped by bellows in the basement, and an English 1820's walnut-topped grand piano. Sir Robert's son, Sir Henry Gore Booth (1843-1900) was a great explorer, and the billiard room how houses artefacts from his yacht *Kara* on which he rescued his friend Leigh Smith from the Arctic ice, and a series of photographs of the Artic presented to him in gratitude by Leigh Smith. It is said that Sir Henry's wife Georgina built the artificial lake at Lissadell in the vain hope that he might stay at home and fish in it, but as the harpoons and whale bones in the billiard room testify, Sir Henry was interested in much larger game.

The sequence of hall and gallery leads straight into the library with its 'great windows' in the garden bow, immortalised by Yeats's poem. The massive and rather unusual chimney-piece of this room, like the others in the main reception rooms, shows the influence of Egyptian Revival. The billiard room now displays family memorabilia, including photographs depicting the life of Constance Markievicz.

The pilasters are painted with a remarkable series of life-sized murals that include the gamekeeper forester and also the butler – the faithful Kilgallon who had accompanied Sir Henry to the Arctic. Sir Henry also brought back the bear that stands stuffed in the front hall. These icon-like murals are the work of Count Casimir Markievicz, the Polish husband of Constance whom she met at the Paris Art School. Her later exploits are well known; she became involved in the Dublin Lockout of 1913, took part in the 1916 rebellion, was imprisoned and later reprieved from a death sentence, became the first elected female Westminster MP, and later served as Minister of Labour in the first Irish government. She died in 1927, a year after the death of Eva, her equally renowned poet sister.

Many of Constance's own artistic efforts line the walls of an exhibition hall dedicated to her life in the restored Coach House, and several illuminated addresses presented to her brother, Sir Josslyn Gore Booth (1869-1944), in recognition of his contribution to the co-operative movement, line the walls of the servants' quarters in the basement of the house. Sir Josslyn, a friend and follower of Horace Plunkett, was responsible for establishing the creameries still operating in Sligo and Leitrim; at Lissadell he developed the resources of the estate, planting enormous numbers of trees, building a sawmill, an engineering works and a sewing school and greatly expanding the vegetable and flower gardens. As part of this policy, an important daffodil nursery was built up which later gave rise to many famous cultivars. Thirty-eight of an original seventy-eight narcissus cultivars developed by Sir Josslyn are now back in the ground at Lissadell.

After 1944 the government assumed responsibility for the administration of the estate when Sir Josslyn's eldest son was made a ward of the court after a nervous breakdown. During this time the estate went

Irish Big Houses

into sharp decline, resulting in the felling of much fine woodland and the compulsory sale in 1968 of 2,600 acres by the Land Commission, leaving only 400 acres around the house.

Located in Ballinfull, 7 miles north of Sligo off the Sligo-Bundoran Road. NGR: G 6346.

COUNTY WATERFORD

Lismore Castle

Everyone who has crossed the bridge over the Blackwater River into the town of Lismore will be familiar with this irresistibly romantic castle, whose splendid silvery-grey turrets, towers and battlements rise serenely from a cliff above the wooded banks of this most Rhine-like of rivers. While extensively remodelled in the nineteenth century, the walls of Lismore incorporate many earlier buildings with a history stretching back over 1,000 years.

Although the name Lios Mor means 'big fort', the castle site was originally occupied by an important monastery and seat of learning established in the early seventh century. It was still an ecclesiastical centre when Henry II stayed here in 1171, and except for a brief period after 1185 when a castle was built here, it served as the episcopal residence of the local bishop. In 1589 Lismore was acquired by Sir Walter Raleigh, who sold the property again in 1602 to another famous adventurer, Richard Boyle, later Earl of Cork. Boyle was a man of extraordinary wealth who had

Lismore Castle, Co. Waterford

arrived in Ireland as a young man in 1588 with only twenty-seven pounds in capital.

He never did anything by halves and having decided to make Lismore his principal seat, proceeded to transform it into a magnificent residence with impressive gabled ranges each side of the court yard. He also made a fortified garden wall with turrets and an outer gatehouse known as the Riding House. The principal apartments were opulently decorated with fretwork plaster ceilings and hangings of tapestry, embroidered silk and velvet. Boyle lived in these apartments with his family and it was here in 1626 that his famous son was born – Robert Boyle, father of modern chemistry. Unfortunately, the castle was sacked by the Confederates in 1645 and although the second Earl made it habitable again, neither he nor his successors, who called themselves by their alternative title of Burlington, were interested in Lismore, preferring to live in England.

Charlotte Boyle, the daughter and heiress of the fourth Earl of Cork, married William Cavendish, fourth Duke of Devonshire in 1748 and through this marriage the castle was inherited by the Cavendish family in 1753. Their son, the fifth Duke (1748-1811), carried out improvements at Lismore, notably the bridge across the Blackwater in 1775, but it was the sixth Duke (1790-1858), known as the Bachelor Duke, who was responsible for the castle's present appearance. He began transforming the castle into a fashionable 'quasi-feudal ultra-regal fortress' as soon as he succeeded his father in 1811, engaging the architect William Atkinson from 1812 to 1822 to rebuild the castle walls with cut stone shipped over from Derbyshire.

The rooms were re-designed with suitably medieval-like Gothic ceilings, the finest undoubtedly in the drawing-room which today contains large tapestries and a magnificent mahogany Irish side-table. This room replaced the old dining room whose 'great window' is said to have caused James II almost to faint when he saw the dramatic drop to the river below. It was during this period of building that workmen discovered the twelfth-century Lismore

Lismore Castle

Crosier, now in the National Museum, Dublin, and the Book of McCarthy Reagh, popularly known as the Book of Lismore, containing important accounts of the lives of Irish saints.

Lismore was always the Bachelor Duke's favourite residence, but as he grew older his love for the place developed into a passion. In 1850 he engaged his architect Sir Joseph Paxton, the designer of the Crystal Palace, to carry out improvements and additions to the castle on a magnificent scale – so much so, indeed, that the present skyline is largely Paxton's work. At this time J.G. Crace of London, the leading makers of Gothic Revival furniture, were commissioned to transform the ruined chapel of the old Bishop's Palace into a medieval-style banqueting hall.

The great architect A.C. Pugin was commissioned to design the room which he left looking rather appropriately like a church, with a huge perpendicular stained glass window, choir-stalls and Gothic stencilling on the walls and roof timbers. The chimney-piece, which was exhibited at the Medieval Court of the Great Exhibition of 1851, was also designed by Pugin (and Myers), but was originally intended for Horstead Place in Sussex, it was rejected because it was too elaborate and subsequently bought for Lismore – the Barchard family emblems later replaced with the present inscription Cead Mille Failte: a hundred thousand welcomes. Pugin also designed other chimney-pieces and furnishings in the castle and after his death in 1851 Crace continued to supply furnishings in the Puginesque manner.

After the Bachelor Duke's death in 1858 the castle was left more or less as he had redesigned it and has fortunately continued to be loved by his successors who still come here for part of the year.

Located in the town of Lismore. NGR: X 043987.

COUNTY WESTMEATH

Belvedere

A desire to escape from the formality of country house life during the eighteenth century led to the emergence of small, comfortable holiday retreats known as villas. Undoubtedly the best example of such a building in Ireland is Belvedere – an exquisite house with an unusual elongated plan set in a fine landscape park overlooking Lough Ennell. Belvedere was built around 1742 to a design by Richard Castle, probably as a fishing pavilion, for Robert Rochfort, Lord Belfield, whose seat at Gaulston lay five miles away. Like other villas of the period, the building was distinguished from ordinary houses of the same size by the exceptionally high quality of its design and construction, most notably its superb joinery and brilliant plasterwork. But the very strange and terrible events that preceded its construction ensured that Belvedere was never really used as a villa, but rather became a country house in its own right.

Belvedere had hardly been completed in 1743 when a great scandal broke out surrounding its builder Robert Rochfort, and his wife Mary Molesworth. She was only sixteen when she married Robert in 1736, but

Belvedere, Co. Westmeath

at the time the match seemed highly suitable; he was intelligent, handsome and one of the country's richest young men, she was the pretty and well-connected daughter of the third Viscount Molesworth. They settled at Gaulston and all seemed well until 1743 when Robert, now Baron Belfield, was informed that his wife had committed adultery with his young brother Arthur, then living near Gaulston at Belfield. Robert, evidently a hot-tempered and self-centred individual, at once removed to his newly completed house at Belvedere, incarcerated his wife at Gaulston and plotted revenge against his brother, who fled to England.

For thirty-one years his wife remained confined at Gaulston with only servants to keep her company. Once in 1756 she managed to escape, but her father refused her entry into his house and within twenty-four hours she was back in Gaulston. Henceforth her movements were further restricted and she was no longer allowed visits by her children. It is said that she used to walk up and down the gallery at Gaulston gazing at the portraits 'as if conversing with them'. After her husband's death in 1774 she was released by her son, who was horrified to find that she had acquired a 'wild, scared, unearthly look, whilst the tones of her voice, which hardly exceeded a whisper, were harsh, agitated and uneven'. As for the unfortunate Arthur, he made the mistake of returning to Ireland in 1759 and was sued for adultery by his unrelenting brother, now Earl of Belvedere. Fined £20,000 in damages, he spent the rest of his life in the Marshalsea, the debtor's jail in Dublin.

Lord Belvedere's treatment of his wife makes gripping reading, but it is also an indictment of eighteenth-century social attitudes. What is so striking is that his behaviour did his reputation no harm at all. At Belvedere he lived an extravagant lifestyle, entertained a great deal and rose through the social ranks to become Earl of Belvedere in 1756 and Master General of the Irish army in 1764.

Belvedere remains much as it was in the Earl's time – a solid grey limestone house of two stories over a basement with a long front and curved end bows, it is probably the earliest bow-ended house in the country. The Venetian and the bow windows provided light for the drawing-room and dining-room at either end of the house and between them are two small rooms (now united as one), a corridor and a handsome wooden staircase in a projection at the back of the building. Both the end rooms are grand but not large, with unusual chamfered corners and very high-quality joinery – their doors, windows and wainscotting all remain unpainted. The drawing-room chimney-piece is a Victorian addition, but other fireplaces and overmantels are original to the house, including a fine example in the east bedroom, probably Lord Belvedere's room.

The delicate rococo plasterwork ceilings are the real glory of Belvedere's interior. Framed by rich cornices these ceilings are notable for their lively quality and freedom of movement. The drawing-room ceiling has scrollwork enclosing medallions of Juno, Minerva and Venus, while that in the dining-room is rather bolder, with clusters of fruit and flowers and four puffing cherubs emerging from clouds in the centre. In the hall the plasterwork is in much lower relief and is supposed to represent the night, with an owl, a flaming torch, stars and more swirling clouds. The name of the plasterer is unknown, but it has been noted that the work closely resembles ceilings formerly at Mespil House outside Dublin; these are believed to have been the work of the Frenchman Bartholomew Cramillion who is known to have made the splendid rococo ceiling in the Rotunda Hospital Chapel in 1755.

Irish Big Houses

The small park that Lord Belvedere created around his villa is just as fine as the house itself and was the envy of all visitors, not least John Wesley who in 1767 remarked that 'one would scarce think it possible to have such a variety of beauties in so small a compass'. One of the attractions was an enormous sham Gothick ruin, which Lord Belvedere in typical fashion built to block out the view of Rochfort House (later known as Tudenham), the home of another of his brothers with whom he had quarrelled. Yet despite his violent and cruel temperament, the Earl was certainly a man of taste and the Gothick arch he had built at the other end of the park is one of the most endearing follies in Ireland.

Following the death of the 'Wicked Earl' (as he was later known) in 1774, the house was inherited by his son, the second Earl, who sold Gaulston and continued to live at Belvedere where he added a small wing to the back. Although his father had left him 'very embarrassed in his circumstances' he managed to revive the family fortunes sufficiently to build a magnificent town residence – now the home of a famous Dublin school. He died without heirs in 1814 and the property was inherited by his sister, the Countess of Lanesborough, and later passed in 1826 to her great-grandson, Charles Brinsley Marley, who lived at Belvedere until his death in 1912. Marley laid out the Italianate terraces in front of the house and assembled a remarkable collection of pictures and objets d'art which was given to Cambridge University upon his death, forming the core of the Fitzwilliam Museum. The residue of this collection together with the house and estate were left to his cousin Lieutenant Colonel C.K. Howard-Bury, leader of the 1921 Mount Everest expedition, who after his death in 1963 bequested it to Rex Beaumont. The contents were auctioned by Christie's in 1980 – a catastrophic loss for any such house.

Happily, the task of safe-guarding Belvedere House and its grounds for the future was undertaken by Westmeath County Council when it was purchased from Beaumont in 1981. An ambitious three-year restoration project, which was co-funded by Failte Ireland, began on the house, the Victorian Walled Garden and the numerous follies including the 'Jealous Wall'. Belvedere House was successfully restored to its Georgian original with Diocletian windows and morning and evening rooms at the entrance. Belvedere opened to the public in May 2000 and attracts many visitors year round.

Located 4 miles from Mullingar on the Tullamore Road. NGR: N 420477.

Tullynally Castle

During the early nineteenth century, a craze for building sham castles spread across Ireland with remarkable speed, undoubtedly provoked by a sense of unease in the aftermath of the 1798 rebellion. Security was certainly a factor in Johnson's 1801 to 1806 remodelling of Tullynally, otherwise known as Pakenham Hall, where practical defensive features such as a portcullis entrance were included in addition to romantic looking battlements and turrets. Later enlargements during the 1820s and 1830s were also fashioned in the castle style and made Tullynally into one of the largest castellated houses in Ireland – so vast, indeed, that it has been compared to a small fortified town.

Masonry walls ten-feet thick are all that remain of the castle that originally stood here in 1655 when Tullynally was purchased by Henry Pakenham, ancestor of the Earls of Longford. By the 1730s this stronghold had been transformed into a grand two-storey house surrounded by extensive formal gardens with canals. Traces of panelling and a few chimney pieces still survive from this building, which was remodelled in 1780 as a five-bay three-storey classical block to the designs of Graham Myers, the architect of Trinity College. It was this building which Francis Johnson, the outstanding architect of his generation in Ireland, was commissioned in 1801 to gothicise for the second Earl of Longford. Johnson designed battlements and label mouldings over the windows, but as work progressed it was felt this treatment was too tame, so between 1805 and 1806 more dramatic features were added, notably round corner turrets and a portcullis entrance, transforming the house with characteristic Irish nomenclature from Pakenham Hall House to Pakenham Hall Castle.

Additions to Johnson's work were made by the second Earl in the early 1820s when James Shiel added a bow on the east garden front and redesigned the entrance hall. More substantial additions followed between 1839 and 1846 when Richard Morrison, that other stalwart of the Irish architectural scene, was employed by the Dowager Countess to bring the house up to improved Victorian standards of convenience. Under Morrison's direction the main house and Johnson's stable court were linked by two parallel wings both of which were elaborately castellated and faced externally with grey limestone. Following the fashion recently made popular by the great Scottish architect William Burn, one of the new wings contained a private apartment for the family, while the other on the east side of the courtyard contained larger and more exactly differentiated servants' quarters with elaborate laundries and a splendid kitchen. After the third Earl's death in 1860 his brother succeeded to the title and property and proceeded to modernise the castle with all the latest equipment for supplying water, heat and lighting. Except for a water tower erected in the stable court by the Dublin architect J. Rawson Carroll in the 1860s, these modifications did not involve altering the fabric of the building, which has remained remarkably unchanged to the present day.

Visitors entering the castle will first arrive in the great hall – an enormous room forty-feet square and thirty-feet high with no gallery to take away from its impressive sense of space. A central-heating system was designed for this room by Richard Lovell Edgeworth, who earlier in 1794 had fitted up the first semaphore telegraph system in Ireland between Edgeworthstown and Pakenham Hall, a distance of twelve miles. In a letter written in December 1807, his daughter Maria Edgeworth, a frequent visitor to Pakenham Hall, wrote that 'the immense hall is so well warmed by hot air that the children play in it from morning to night. Lord L. seemed to take great pleasure in repeating twenty times that he was to thank Mr. Edgeworth for this.' Edgeworth's heating system was, in fact, so effective that when Shiel remodelled the hall in 1820 he replaced one of the two fireplaces with a built-in organ that visitors can still see. James Shiel was also responsible for the Gothic vaulting of the ceiling, the Gothic niches containing the family crests, the high wood panelling around the base of the walls and the massive cast-iron Gothic fireplace. Other features of the room include a number of attractive early nineteenth-century drawings of the castle, a collection of old weapons, family portraits and an Irish elk's head dug up out of a bog once a familiar feature of Irish country house halls.

The drawing room which retains its appearance from Johnson's remodelling of the house, including a decorated ceiling in the geometric manner. This is a pleasant room, with canvases of sea battles, a Chinese cabinet handpainted by an Irishman and a dinner service donated to Admiral Sir Thomas Pakenham by grateful German merchants rescued from pirates. The adjacent library, which also has magnificent views over rolling parkland, is a spacious and comfortable room; oak bookcases tower from floor to ceiling and a delightful alcove stands in one corner. Over the mantelpiece is a portrait of the second Earl's brother, Sir Edward Pakenham, a Peninsular War general who later lost his life at the Battle of New Orleans in the War of 1812. The distinguished military past of the Pakenhams has

Tullynally Castle

been replaced this century by an equally distinguished literary tradition. Family members include the present Earl of Longford, who has written numerous books including the lives of Nixon and de Valera; his wife Elizabeth, who has written important biographies of the Duke of Wellington and Queen Victoria; their son Thomas Pakenham, author of highly acclaimed accounts of the 1798 rebellion, the South African War and the colonial struggle for Africa; his sister Antonia Fraser, another distinguished biographer, and Rachel Billington, a novelist.

One of the most fascinating features of Tullynally Castle is surely the rooms belowstairs. Visitors can tour the splendid kitchen with its great ovens, a great pestle and mortar, an early ice chest and a dresser with gleaming brassware probably bought for the kitchen when it was built in the 1840s. Sadly, because this kitchen remained in continuous use its huge 1875 range was replaced by an Aga in the 1940s. Other rooms of special interest include the Victorian laundries, which remain largely as they were after being remodelled between 1863 and 1864 by the fourth Earl. Here the inquisitive will find a wash house with lead-lined sinks and a giant mangle with a heavy roller used for sheets, an ironing room (now used as a tea room) and a drying-room fitted up with vertical racks on rails that could be pulled in and out of a heated chamber. Some of the drying, however, had to be done in an open-air drying-yard beyond the stables; this was approached by a sunken passage allowing the laundry maids (who were apt to be pretty) to carry the washing to the yard without having to meet any of the grooms on the way.

Located 1 mile outside of Castlepollard on the Granard Road, 13 miles from Mullingar.
NGR: N 445705.

COUNTY WICKLOW

Russborough

Irish country houses are generally distinguished by their architecture rather than their contents, but Russborough is a striking exception to this rule. Not only does this magnificent Palladian mansion boast lavish plasterwork, splendid chimney-pieces and superb joinery, but it also contains a selection from the world-famous Beit collection of pictures, furniture and objets d'art. It can justifiably be said that Russborough, with its superb landscape setting, is indeed a temple of the art – a place of rare quality and beauty.

The house was commissioned by Joseph Lesson, later the first Earl of Milltown (1705-83), after inheriting the wealth of his father, an opulent Dublin brewer. Completion of the building which began in 1741 took over ten years so that the designer, Richard Castle (1690-1751) never lived to see the final stages that were carried out by his associate Francis Bindon. The house is built of local silver-grey granite with wonderfully crisp detail and has an entrance front that extends to 700 feet, the longest in Ireland. The centre block of seven bays and two stories over a basement is relatively small, but is extended over via colonnaded quadrant wings to seven-bay, two-storey pavilions. Further out stretch high plain walls, each broken by a centrally placed rustic arch terminating in one-storey pavilions associated with the kitchen and stableyards. Fortune has smiled kindly upon Russborough for it has remained free of subsequent alterations, with most of Castle's original features surviving intact.

Ascending the broad flight of granite steps guarded by a pair of carved lions, the visitor enters the front hall – a well-proportioned room with a floor of polished oak and an ornate but severe compartmental ceiling with Doric frieze quite similar to the one Castle designed for Leinster House. The monumental chimney-piece is of black Kilkenny marble, much favoured by Castle for entrance halls, while above it hangs a striking painting by Oudry of Indian Black-buck with Pointers and Still Life, dated 1745. Five doors with magnificently carved architraves of West Indian mahogany lead to the major reception rooms: the saloon, the drawing-room, the dining-room, the tapestry room and the grand staircase.

Undoubtedly the finest room in the house is the saloon, which occupies the three central bays of the north front. It has a coved ceiling with rococo plasterwork incorporating flowers, garlands, swags and putti, which on stylistic grounds can be attributed to the Francini brothers of Italy. The walls are covered with a crimson cut Genoese velvet dating from around 1840 –an ideal background for paintings which include many pictures from the Beit collection. The room also has Louis XVI furniture in Gobelins tapestry signed by Pluvinet, a pair of Japanese lacquer cabinets from Harewood House and a chimney-piece identical to one at Uppark in Sussex, which must be the work of Thomas Carter (the younger) of London.

A striking feature of the room is the inlaid sprung mahogany floor with a central star in satinwood. This was covered with a green baize drugget when the house was occupied by rebels during the 1798 rebellion. The potential of the drugget for making four fine flags was considered but rejected by the rebels, lest 'their brogues might ruin his lordship's floor'. The rebels, in fact, did virtually no damage to the house during their stay, although the government forces who occupied the building afterwards were considerably less sympathetic. It is said that the troops only left in 1801 after a furious Lord Milltown challenged Lord Tyrawley to a duel 'with underbusses and slugs in a sawpit'.

Flanking the saloon along the northern front is the music room and the library, formerly the dining-room, both framed by ebullient rococo ceiling that were probably also the work of the Francini brothers. The coffered and richly decorated barrel-vaulted ceiling of the tapestry room, to the south of the music room, is by a less experienced artist, though the room is no less impressive than the others and contains an English state bed made in London in 1795 and two Soho tapestries of Moghul subjects by Vanderbank. Infused with a restless energy the plasterwork in the adjacent drawing-room spills onto the walls,

Russsborough, Co. Wicklow

where fantastic plaster frames surround the four oval marine scenes by Vernet representing morning, noon, evening and night. Although part of the patrimony of the house, these pictures were sold in 1926 and only after a determined search were recovered forty-three years later by Sir Alfred Beit. Beyond lies the doudoir – a charming little panelled apartment with a Bossi chimney-piece dating around 1780. From here visitors pass into the tapestry-hung corridor leading to the pavilion, formerly the bachelor's quarters. The dining-room, formerly the library, on the opposite side of the hall has a monumental Irish chimney-piece of mottled grey Sicilian, marble. The walls are ornamented both by paintings from the Beit collection and two magnificent Louis XIV tapestries.

No one who visits Russborough is likely to forget the staircase with its extraordinary riot of exuberant plasterwork; there is nothing quite like it anywhere else in the British Isles. In later years the decorator Mr Sibthorpe is reported to have remarked that it represented 'the ravings of a maniac', adding that he was 'afraid the madman was Irish'.

On the death of the sixth Earl of Milltown in 1890, Russborough passed to his widow and later to his nephew before being sold out of the family in 1931. Fortunately, most of its famous art collection assembled by the first Earl remained in Ireland when the sixth Earl's widow bequeathed it to the National Gallery of Ireland in 1902 – a bequest so important that a new wing was built to contain it. Russborough was not devoid of art treasure for long, however; the property was acquired by Sir Alfred Beit in 1951 as the setting for one of the world's most outstanding private art collections. Dominated by Dutch, Flemish and Spanish masterpieces, this collection was largely formed by Alfred Beit (1853-1906), a co-founder with Cecil Rhodes of the De Beers Diamond Mining Company in South Africa. The house and part of the collection have now been given to a foundation and are open to the public. The remainder of the paintings have been donated to the National Gallery of Ireland. It is unique in Ireland that one house, Russborough, has provided two separate and distinguished art collections to the State. In recognition of this fact the National Gallery has two wings named after the benefactors being the 'Milltown' wing and separately the 'Beit' wing. In addition Russborough remains as one of the most beautiful houses in Ireland.

Located 2 1/2 miles south west of Blessington. NGR: N 957100.

Muckross House, Co. Kerry

Acknowledgements

The publisher would like to thank the following for permission to reproduce work in copyright:

© The Alfred Beit Foundation (p123)
© Barry Mason (p126)
© The Trustees of Muckross House (Killarney) Ltd (p64)
© Irish Heritage Trust (p25)
© Beaulieu House, Gardens & Car Museum (p86)
© Kylemore Abbey (p61)
© Westport House (pp4 and 90)
© Belvedere House (p111)
© Strokestown Park House (p98)
© Clare County Council. Photograph by Sonia Schorman. (p19)
© Catherine Casey, Heritage Officer, Laois County Council (p76)
© The National Trust. Photographs by Roger Kinkead (pp9, 13, 30)
© The National Trust. Photographs by Christopher Hill (pp51, 56, 81)
© The National Trust. Photograph by Mike Williams (p36)
© istockphoto.com/Richard Cano (p42)
© istockphoto.com/Joe Gough (p107)
© Bantry House (pp6 and 21)
© Lissadell Collection. Photograph by Steve Rogers (p102)

Index

Ardress	8
Argory, The	12
Bantry House	20
Beaulieu	85
Belvedere	110
Castle Coole	49
Castle Ward	29
Castletown House	68
Clonalis House	95
Emo Court	75
Florence Court	55
Fota House, Arboretum and Gardens	24
Kylemore Abbey	60
Lismore Castle	106
Lissadell House	101
Malahide Castle	41
Mount Ievers Court	17
Mount Stewart	35
Muckross House	63
Newbridge House	45
Russborough	120

Springhill	80
Strokestown Park House	97
Tullynally Castle	116
Westport House	89